DATE DUE

DEMCO 38-296

CARL RUGGLES

Photograph of Carl Ruggles courtesy of Archives of American Art, Smithsonian Institution, Artists Collection I.

CARL RUGGLES

A Bio-Bibliography

Jonathan D. Green

Bio-Bibliographies in Music, Number 59
Donald L. Hixon, Series Adviser

GREENWOOD PRESS
Westport, Connecticut • London

Library of Congress Cataloging-in-Publication Data

Green, Jonathan D.
    Carl Ruggles : a bio-bibliography / Jonathan D. Green.
        p.   cm.—(Bio-bibliographies in music, ISSN 0742–6968   ;   no.
    59)
      Discography: p.
      Includes index.
      ISBN 0–313–29456–9 (alk. paper)
      1. Ruggles, Carl, 1876–1971—Bibliography.   I. Title.
    II. Series.
    ML134.R84G74   1995
    780′.92 —dc20
    [B]   95–38559

British Library Cataloguing in Publication Data is available.

Library of Congress Catalog Card Number: 95–38559
ISBN: 0–313–29456–9
ISSN: 0742–6968

First published in 1995

Greenwood Press, 88 Post Road West, Westport, CT 06881
An imprint of Greenwood Publishing Group, Inc.

Printed in the United States of America

The paper used in this book complies with the
Permanent Paper Standard issued by the National
Information Standards Organization (Z39.48–1984).

10 9 8 7 6 5 4 3 2 1

This book is dedicated to Lionel H. Nowak, friend and champion of the subject, and an inspiration to the author.

CONTENTS

PREFACE

That Carl Ruggles holds an important place in the history of American music is unarguable, but his place, however significant, is very small. From his ninety-five years, evidence of only twenty-five works remains, and of these, the composer only sanctioned eight. The entire duration of these eight works is about one hour, and even a few minutes of that hour rarely find their way into concert halls. Ruggles wrote little prose, held no prominent academic post, nor did he have a prominent career as a performer. He spent most of the second half of his long life in the seclusion of the Vermont mountains sheltered from the public eye. For all of these reasons there is little material from or about this enigmatic composer, but what does exist reveals a truly remarkable talent.

In the years following the composer's death, little was written about him outside of a few theory journals until around 1990 when he began to reappear as the subject of graduate research. Since that time a number of new digital recordings have also been made of some of the smaller works. With the advent of new-found interest in Ruggles, this study seems most appropriate.

The biography chapter presents a chronological account of Ruggles's life and career. This chapter utilizes materials listed in the chapters that follow: "Works and Performances" (**W** numbers), "Discography" (**D** numbers), "Ruggles as Author" (**A** numbers), "Bibliography of Ruggles" (**B** numbers), "Unpublished Writings on Ruggles" (**Bunp** numbers), "Theses and Dissertations" (**Th** numbers), "Programs of Concerts" (**Pro** numbers), "Miscellany" (**M** numbers), and "Collections of Archival Materials" (**C** numbers).

The second chapter, "Works and Performances," using the mnemonic **W** followed by a catalogue number, lists all of Ruggles's known compositions (**W1-W25**). Those works which were completed and published are listed first, in chronological order

(**W1-W8**). For these, the publisher, duration, dedications, and instrumentation are listed. If a work was published in two different versions, the catalogue number is followed by **/1** or **/2** to distinguish them. Selected performances of each work are catalogued chronologically after the work's main listing, using the work's number followed a lower-case letter (i.e., **W3a**). Cross-references are given below each entry for applicable recordings (**D** numbers), reviews and analyses (**B** and **Th** numbers), etc.

The third chapter, "Discography," using the mnemonic **D**, lists all recordings of Ruggles's compositions (**D1-D20**). These entries include performers, dates of recording (when known), and record serial numbers. Entries are followed with cross-references to other chapters using the appropriate mnemonic and catalogue number.

The fourth chapter, "Ruggles as Author," using the mnemonic **A**, lists citations of music reviews published by the composer (**A1-A2**).

The fifth chapter, "General Bibliography," uses the mnemonics **B, Bunp, Th, Pro**, and **M** as follows: Journal and Newspaper Articles (**B1-B85**), Citations in Books (**B86-B217**), Book on Ruggles (**B218**), Unpublished Materials (**Bunp1-Bunp6**), Theses and Dissertations (**Th1-Th10**), Concert Programs (**Pro1-Pro3**), Miscellany (**M1-M2**). Each of these is followed by cross-references where appropriate.

The sixth chapter, "Collections of Archival Materials," using the mnemonic **C**, lists repositories of original archival materials relevant to the composer (**C1a-C11**).

The "Index" lists all authors, articles, books, serials, compositions, and subjects. Authors, articles, books, serials, and compositions are cited by mnemonic and catalogue number of the principal entry. Subjects are listed by mnemonic and catalogue number for all relevant entries. All index entries cited to the "Biography" chapter are listed by actual page number.

ACKNOWLEDGMENTS

I first encountered the music of Carl Ruggles in a composition lesson with Robert Stern. Two years later, I had the distinct pleasure of serving as the music librarian at Bennington College for the 1987-1988 academic year. There, composers Lionel Nowak, Lou Calabro, and Vivian Fine each shared stories of their associations with Ruggles. Their collective enthusiasm about his music entreated me to delve into all of his works and his unusual career. That has circuitously led to this current study.

I have been invaluably assisted by Mr. Ted Hunter of the Music Listening Center at the University of North Carolina at Greensboro, and by the library staff of Elon College, especially former head librarian, Dr. P. Alston Jones, Jr., Ms. Teresa LePors, Ms. Diana Engel, and Mr. Eric Childress. Suzanne Jones of Bennington College sent me copies of a number of useful unpublished items. My wife, Lynn Buck, has offered much helpful criticism. To all of the above I owe many heartfelt thanks.

It is also a privilege to offer thanks to the series editor, Mr. Don Hixon, for his patience and sage advice.

CARL RUGGLES

BIOGRAPHY

Life

During the 1920s had Edgard Varèse or Charles Ives been asked to name America's greatest living composer, barring any narcissistic inclination, the response would have been: "Carl Ruggles." Forty years later such eminent experts on American music as Nicolas Slonimsky, Virgil Thomson and Aaron Copland would each describe Ruggles as our most technically refined composer. Though it is true that Ruggles's name was surely never a general household commodity, he, with Varèse and Ives, was the standard bearer of the atonal movement in this century's third decade. Today, excepting a few scattered performances of *Angels* and *Evocations*, Ruggles's small, but potent repertoire rests silently; and his name is recognized by a few who remember him only as a New England iconoclast who lived in a schoolhouse and enjoyed sharing his scatological humor.

Carl Ruggles's music is of a distinct and personal style which is the result of a most exacting compositional technique. His entire published output is about eighty minutes in length. Ruggles is in many ways America's Webern. Although Webern's works have an unduly limited audience, his legacy as a composer remains strong through its intertwining with Berg and Schoenberg. Ruggles, on the other hand, stood as an island and lacking the support of a musical archipelago, he has faded quickly from our nation's cultural memory.

Born Charles Sprague Ruggles on 11 March 1876 in Marion, Massachusetts (near Buzzard's Bay), the second of three children, to an old New England family, Ruggles showed an early interest in music. As a child, he fashioned a violin from a cigar box. This contraption was soon replaced with a more conventional instrument donated by the local lighthouse keeper. He was apparently a gifted beginner playing duets with Mrs. Grover Cleveland who vacationed in the area. Ruggles's mother died in 1890, so the boy and his father moved to Lexington for nearly a year, and then settled in Waverly. In this period of moving around Carl apparently dropped out of high school.

Around the turn of the century, Ruggles studied music theory with Josef Claus who was a European emigré on the faculty of the Boston Conservatory of Music. At this time, he also studied the violin with Felix Winternitz. It was about this time that he began calling himself Carl believing it to sound more Germanic, therefore reflecting his inclinations in musical taste. In 1903, Carl took an English composition class as a special student at Harvard. He studied music composition privately with John Knowles Paine who also happened to be on the Harvard faculty (**B83**).

In 1907, the Mar d'Mar Music School in Winona, Minnesota invited Ruggles to join its faculty as instructor of violin. In the following year, the singer Charlotte Snell, with whom Ruggles had become enamored in Massachusetts, moved to Winona to become his bride. Charlotte Ruggles soon became a singing teacher at the Mar d'Mar School. During this same year, Ruggles organized the Winona Symphony, a community orchestra which met at the YMCA. The local musicians were joined by members of the St. Paul Symphony, most notably its concertmaster, Christian Timner. Mr. Timner had been Mengelberg's concertmaster of the Concertgebouw Orchestra in Amsterdam. During the four years that Ruggles led the Winona group he was coached privately in his conducting by the more worldly Timner.

During this time in Minnesota, Ruggles composed a number of songs and small works which he later removed from his catalogue. He also had begun work on an opera entitled *The Sunken Bell* (**W9**). It used a libretto by Charles Henry Meltzer, a distinguished critic who also translated many operas into English. The libretto was based upon the play *Die versunkene Glocke* by Gerhart Robert Hauptmann, which Meltzer had previously translated as a straight play (**M2**). Carl discontinued his work with the orchestra in 1912 so that he could more fully dedicate his energies to the opera. He still gave violin lessons, and Charlotte maintained her voice studio and continued to direct the choir of the local Congregational church.

Word of *The Sunken Bell* had roused the interest of the Opera in Our Language Foundation whose aim it was to establish opera in English in the United States. In 1917, hopeful that a production at the Metropolitan Opera was possible, Ruggles moved to New York where he continued his operatic work. Charlotte and their two-year-old son, Micah, remained in Minnesota until the following year.

Ruggles soon became friends with Eugene Schoen, an architect, who arranged for Carl to be hired by the Rand School of Social Science to form and direct a workers' orchestra. Progress with the new group was slow, but after their first concert, Carl's duties were expanded to include directing the chorus. In 1920, Carl was made director of the Rand School's new music department. In the spring of the following year, the school's board of directors elected to eliminate the ensembles, and so ended Carl's association with the Rand School (**B218**).

At about the same time, Ruggles abandoned the opera, though the work was apparently near completion. He destroyed much of it and only fragments now survive (**Th5**). There are a number of accounts that suggest that the opera was withdrawn when the Metropolitan Opera refused to have a special bell cast for the production, wishing to substitute a papier-mâché bell, but this story seems unlikely and cannot be substantiated. The composer claimed that its withdrawal was due to the fact that the text was a translation, and hence impure. The withdrawal also coincided with the crystallization of his compositional style, and it seems likely that the opera did not correspond to his new criteria.

In any case the time spent on *The Sunken Bell* was very much the equivalent of an apprenticeship. At this point Carl also rejected his previous compositions with the exception of *Toys* (**W1**), a short song which he composed for Micah's fourth birthday using his own text:

> Come here, little son, and I will play with you.
> See, I have brought you lovely toys—
> Painted ships,
> And trains of choo choo cars, and a wondrous
> balloon, that floats, and floats, and floats, way up to
> the stars.

In this song Ruggles's style can be seen to be taking shape. It is very concise with elegant control of fairly dissonant lines while using no superfluous activity within an efficient accompaniment. It was through this song that Carl came in contact with the International Composers' Guild and its founders Edgard Varèse and Carlos Salzedo. Much to Carl's surprise, he could find no one to perform *Toys* until it caught the attention of Varèse who soon invited Carl to join the Guild. So began Ruggles's long association with the Guild and his longer friendship with Varèse. *Toys* received its premiere on a 1923 concert of the Guild (**W1a**).

Carl's first work to appear in a Guild concert (**W2/1a**) was *Angels* (**W2/1**) for six muted trumpets in 1922. *Angels* was composed in 1920 and was originally intended as the second movement of a three-movement work, *Men and Angels* (**W14**), which without *Angels* was reworked into *Men and Mountains* (**W4/1**). It marks the beginning of Ruggles's most productive period and the establishment of his reputation as a significant composer.

Varèse arranged for *Toys* to be published by H. W. Gray (1920) and *Angels* (1925) by Curwen, both English music houses. Interestingly, the *Angels* score includes an organ transcription of the work by Lynnwood Farnam (**W2/3**).

The year 1924 saw the premieres of *Vox clamans in deserto* (**W3**), three songs for voice and chamber ensemble, and *Men and Mountains* (**W4/1**), both on Guild concerts (**W3a, W4/1a**).

It was also in 1924 that Carl and Charlotte moved to Arlington, Vermont, where they purchased a one-room school house which they converted into their summer home. That same year Harriette Miller, a New York philanthropist, decided to become the patroness of Arlington. Dismayed by the community's New England stoicism and lack of interest, she therefore chose instead to support one member of the community. This member was the newly immigrated Ruggles who gladly became the recipient of a life-long annuity. During the next twelve years, the Ruggles lived between Arlington and New York.

In 1920 Carl had befriended composers Henry Cowell and Charles Seeger. Cowell selected *Men and Mountains* for the inaugural edition in 1927 of his landmark serial, *New Music Quarterly*. Cowell had secured 594 subscriptions to this new journal which was made up of scores of modern music. Reaction of the subscribers was mixed, and nearly half of the first editions were returned. A member of the advisory board for the New Music Society was Charles Ives. He purchased the returned copies to help save Cowell's foundling venture. This bail-out was also a gesture of support for the music of Ruggles who was soon to become a close friend of Ives. *Men and Mountains* was included on a program of the Chamber Orchestra of Boston under Nicolas Slonimsky in New York's Town Hall with the premiere of Ives's *Three Places in New England* (**W4/1b**). During both works the audience hissed and heckled. Ives silently tolerated his own work being berated, but when a man near him began to heckle Carl's piece, he exclaimed:

"Stop being such a God-damned sissy! When you hear masculine music like this, you've got to stand up and use your ears like a man (**B127**)!"

In 1925 Carl completed *Portals* (**W5**) for thirteen solo strings. It was premiered the following year under Eugene Goosens as part of the Guild's season (**W5a**). *Portals* was re-scored for string orchestra in thirteen independent parts in 1929. This version received it premiere in Carnegie Hall in a performance by the Conductorless Orchestra (**W5b**).

Ruggles's next composition was his magnum opus, *Sun-Treader* (**W6**). This eighteen minute work for large orchestra was completed in 1931. It is in a modified ternary form, as are most of Ruggles's works, and is contrapuntally conceived from beginning to end. In 1931, Slonimsky had conducted two concerts of American avant-garde music in the Salle Gaveau in Paris which included *Men and Mountains* and works of Ives, Varèse, and Cowell. He returned to Paris the following year to conduct the Orchestre Symphonique de Paris in a program that included the premiere of *Sun-Treader* (**W6a**). Rehearsals were reportedly tense, with Varèse who was present as a sponsor assuaging his fellow countrymen and convincing them to give the music a chance (**B66**). Slonimsky wired to Ives for extra funds to provide additional rehearsal time. Ives immediately sent a check. Two years later, Ives also significantly underwrote the cost of engraving for the first edition of *Sun-Treader*. The premiere of *Sun-Treader* was a success and a number of subsequent performances were given throughout Europe in the following few years in cities which included Vienna, Berlin, Prague, and Madrid, but it was not until 1966 that it would be performed in the composer's native land (**W6b**). It would be another two years after that American premiere until Ruggles had the opportunity to hear his masterpiece performed (**W6d**), and this would be via loud speaker to his nursing-home bedroom.

The Great Depression had a profound effect upon music and musical organizations in the United States. The International Composers' Guild reorganized to become the Pan-American Association of Composers prolonging its life in those economically troubled times, but the organization ultimately folded in 1936. The musical interests of the nation turned toward a more accessible style. Some composers followed these winds of change; still, a handful of the ultra-moderns, Ruggles among them, remained true to their beliefs and methods while falling out of public view (**Th3**). It was clearly a time of transition.

In Arlington, Ruggles had become acquainted with many of that village's creative residents including the novelist, Dorothy Canfield Fischer, and the illustrators Rockwell Kent, John Atherton and Norman Rockwell. During a trip to Jamaica in 1935, Ruggles took up painting; a fascination for it was surely fired by his legendary friends. This interest became cemented when Kent wagered that he could more easily compose music than Carl could paint. Ruggles won, and his works now hang in many galleries, including the Brooklyn Museum, Detroit Institute of Art, and the Whitney Gallery. It is worth noting that in Kent's much acclaimed illustrations for *Moby Dick*, Ruggles serves as the model for Captain Ahab.

In 1934, Micah entered the University of Miami at Coral Gables, Florida. Since moving to Vermont, the Ruggleses had spent their winters in New York. In 1936 they chose warm Miami to be their winter home. They could avoid the harsh Arlington winters and be near their son. Carl was invited to teach part-time in the School of Music at the University that winter. He presented a seminar on modern music which required permission of the instructor for admission. He also taught a few composition lessons. It was for a performance of a student ensemble (**W2/2a**) that Carl re-scored *Angels* for trumpets and trombones(**W2/2**).

During this period in his life, Ruggles began spending more of his time painting, but he did compose *Evocations* (**W7**) and began *Organum* (**W8**) during those Miami years. He held the teaching post until 1944 when he retired permanently to Arlington.

Evocations is subtitled "Four Chants for Piano." These pieces were composed between 1937 and 1944, and are dedicated respectively to his patroness, Harriette Miller; pianist, John Kirkpatrick; his wife, Charlotte; and friend, Charles Ives. The first and last of these pieces (in their final order) were premiered by Kirkpatrick, who had also presented the first public performance of Ives's *Concord Sonata*, in 1940 in a private recital (**W7a**). Three of the pieces were given by Kirkpatrick in a Town Hall recital in January of 1942. After all four of the pieces were completed, Carl continued to revise them until a new edition was made available in 1954.

Organum was completed in 1945 and was premiered by the New York Philharmonic in Carnegie Hall under Leopold Stokowski in 1949 (**W8a**). Stokowski led a number of subsequent performances with various orchestras (**B114**). This marked the end of Ruggles's new works. He spent the remainder of his days revising his works: perfecting the seemingly perfect.

The rise of social realism in the 1930s had brought an end to Ruggles's notoriety, but during his retirement, he began to receive long overdue recognition. In 1954, he was elected to the National Institute of Arts and Letters. He also received an honorary Doctor of Music degree from the University of Vermont in 1960 as the state celebrated "Carl Ruggles Day." Ruggles was also presented with the Creative Arts Medal by Brandeis University in 1964.

In 1957, Charlotte died. Carl would often be heard saying, "I was never worthy of her." Perhaps from grief, he was moved to compose one more piece in 1957: *Exaltation* (**B13**), an accompanied hymn for congregation in unison. This piece has little in common with Ruggles's other works. Using the text of "Our God, Our Help in Ages Past," and the tune *St. Anne* as a point of departure, it is a beautiful, and most sincere tribute of a loving husband for his lost love. As Ruggles's career began with a birthday ode for his young son, so it would close with a memorial to his bride.

As Ruggles entered his ninetieth year, he became a *cause célèbre*. Bowdoin College held a "Carl Ruggles Festival" which included the American premiere of *Sun-Treader* by the Boston Symphony in Portland, Maine. Having been cautioned against excessive travel, the composer was unable to attend and fortuitously avoided a sudden blizzard.

In 1968, thirty-six years after its Parisian debut, Ruggles finally heard a performance of his *Sun-Treader* as his complete works were performed in Bennington, Vermont. Ruggles had moved to Bennington so that he could enter a health-care facility. This festival concert was performed by the Bennington Community Orchestra, the Vermont State Symphony, the Berkshire Symphony, the Northeastern New York Philharmonia, and members of the Bennington College Faculty. Guest Speakers for this concert included George Hughes, Eric Salzman, Peter Yates, and John Kirkpatrick. During the program, Ruggles was presented with the 1968 Vermont Governor's Award for Excellence in the Arts, which was given in absentia as the composer listened to the concert through a speaker which had been wired into his bedroom. He feared becoming overly emotional during the program, but was visited by many of the performers the following day with whom he discussed the program thoroughly (**W6d, Pro2**).

Carl Ruggles died 24 October 1971 in Bennington, at the age of ninety-five.

Works

All of Ruggles's music is cut from the same heavy musical cloth. It is a fabric much like that of pre-serial Schoenberg, but more carefully woven, more refined. Ruggles's is a music of constant and carefully-controlled dissonance. It is exactingly contrapuntal in construction yet consistently atonal. His music is constructed linearly, harmony being the mere result of properly juxtaposed voices. Though never truly serial, each independent voice will usually sound eight to ten different chromatic pitches before a pitch is repeated. Unlike the Viennese atonalists, Ruggles did not treat traditionally enharmonic pitches as equal, but carefully calculated his use of specific accidentals. Ruggles's constant dedication to the independence of voices, and the need for melodic integrity in all parts, rings as an atonal echo of Bach.

Ruggles seems to have been less concerned with orchestration than any other compositional matter, as can be seen in the variety of timbral choices made available by his indications in *Angels*, the first score of which indicated that a performance could be given on any six instruments of like timbres. Ruggles's orchestrational energies were directed toward absolute clarity in the presentation of the counterpoint. Formally, he had a proclivity for modified ternary form wherein the return of the opening material is modified most frequently by a concision of melodic material and an expansion in the voicing of the parts (B131).

Excluding *Exaltation* (**W13**) and *Men and Angels* (**W14**) which have been recorded, but not published, Ruggles left behind eight excruciatingly well-crafted pieces ranging in forces from piano and voice to mammoth orchestra, and in length from one-and-a-half to eighteen minutes. Ruggles, like his friend Ives, was deeply moved by the poetry of the nineteenth century. Most of his works bear poetical inscriptions from the Romantics.

Toys (**W1**), for soprano and piano, was composed for Micah Ruggles's fourth birthday on a text by the composer. This, with the exception of *Exaltation*, is the least characteristic of his works, but it is a most endearing display of a father's love for his son. The vocal range is exceptionally wide, allowing the dense textures of the piano and the precocious vocal line to remain distinct from one another.

Angels (**W2/1**), originally for five trumpets and bass trumpet, was revised in 1940 (**W2/2**) for four trumpets and three trombones (in either case muted). Ultimately, the composer indicated that any seven instruments of like timbre may be employed. This is the epitome of sublimity in music as the seemingly static texture of the muted brass shifts from one dissonance to another arching to a climax of more pointed dissonance gradually reposing to the more placid dissonance of its beginning.

Vox clamans in deserto (**W3**) for soprano and chamber orchestra is in three movements: 1) "Parting at Morning" (Robert Browning), 2) "Son of Mine" (Charles Henry Meltzer), 3) "A Clear Midnight" (Walt Whitman). In these songs, named by Henry Cowell, the voice is surrounded by the "desert" environment of the orchestra which envelopes the singer in an electrified haze of dissonance through which she utters a hauntingly expressive melody. There is another unfinished song entitled "Sea Pattern," setting Whitman's poem "As if a Phantom Caress'd Me," which was originally intended for this set (**W17**). These songs were withdrawn for many years, apparently in reaction to a poor first performance (B66), but have been restored to Ruggles's catalogue in a new edition from Theodore Presser.

Men and Mountains (**W4/1**), for small orchestra, was revised for large orchestra in 1936 and 1940 (**W4/2**). It is in three movements: 1) "Men," 2) "Lilacs (for string orchestra only)," and 3) "Marching Mountains." The work is prefaced with a quotation of William Blake, "Great things are done when men and mountains meet." The work is purely polyphonic with leap-filled craggy lines which bound with intense virility toward stratospheric climaxes. Even the middle movement, which may owe its title to Whitman's funereal "When Lilacs Last in the Dooryard Bloom'd," is a hardy and direct piece. No moment of this work falls into a mire of affectation.

Portals (**W5**) for full string orchestra contains contrapuntal writing that sometimes extends into thirteen independent parts. The work is prefaced by a line from Whitman: "What are those of the known but to ascend and enter the unknown?" Ruggles's poetic allusion here, as in *Angels*, is not as a literal tone poem, but rather the evocation of the poetic mood. As in the tradition of Brahms, his references are atmospheric and emotional rather than representational. It is in this work that Ruggles exercises the most specific control of the performance. With the possible exception *Sun-Treader*; the score is more laden with indications of tempo, articulation, and dynamics than in his other works. His dynamic range is extreme from very soft to triple forte. The work is permeated by a remarkable, unrelenting tension that drives it to a remarkably powerful climax.

Sun-Treader (**W6**) for very large orchestra is Ruggles's grandest undertaking in terms of its length and orchestrational scope. In the words of Arthur Cohn, "Ruggles's music represents chromaticism in its most striated state. His orchestration is beautifully 'incorrect' and thereby artistically unadulterated. Its imbalance and muddiness present orchestrational audacity, sonorous hyperbole, and yet it conveys the musical idea exactly (**B106**)." Due to the immense size of the ensemble required for this work, it is rarely heard, and yet it remains Ruggles's most celebrated work.

In *Evocations: Four Chants for Piano* (**W7**) the jagged qualities of Ruggles's counterpoint become most apparent when confined to the keyboard. Here, without the possibility of instrumental doubling, his independent voicings become more exposed and have been interpreted by some critics as constricted and somewhat clumsy (**B100**). An interesting feature of these pieces is their use of unusual sustaining features and harmonics. Although these pieces do not bear poetic inscriptions, they reflect a musico-poetic intent. The four pieces are thoroughly dissonant, having remarkable forward momentum resulting from the unfulfilled expectation of repose.

Organum (**W8**) for orchestra was first performed in an arrangement for two pianos (**W16a**). Upon first glance, *Organum* resembles an exercise in sixteenth-century counterpoint. With further inspection it becomes clear that this is a piece of scrupulously organized dissonance owing its linear architecture to Renaissance models, but remaining entrenched in the composer's familiar scheme of atonality.

The brevity of Ruggles's oeuvre with respect to his incredible longevity is, at first, surprising. He was seven years old when Wagner died, and he passed away the year the Beatles separated. Virgil Thomson stated that in creating music of such fastidious craft and musical concision, Ruggles could not have composed more (**B203**). There is a consistency and sublime refinement in his compositions which is without equal in American music. Within Ruggles's works are some of this century's finest achievements in the art of composition, a legacy which lays waiting to be restored to its rightful station in the world's concert halls.

WORKS AND PERFORMANCES

W1   **Toys** (1919, H.W. Gray, 2 minutes)

soprano and piano
Text: Carl Ruggles

Ruggles composed this song for his son's fourth birthday, 25 May 1919. The cover page was designed by Rockwell Kent, with Kent's signature actually written in by the composer.

The work is dedicated "To my little son Micah."

[See: D1, D7, B37, B38, B39, B66, B69, B75, B100, B125, B126, B131, B132, B134, B135, B151, B163, B168, B179, B203, B206, B218, Th1, Th7, Th8, C1a]

Premiere

W1a   1923 (4 March): New York, NY; Klaw Theatre; Third concert of the International Composers Guild season; Lucy Gates, soprano.

[see: B218]

Other Selected Performances

W1b   1968 (29 September): Bennington, VT; Mount Anthony Union High School; "Carl Ruggles Festival," a concert of the complete published works in conjunction with an exhibit of his paintings. Bethany Beardslee, soprano; Vivian Fine, piano.

[see: W2/2d, W3b, W4/2f, W5j, W6d, W7i, W8c, B42,B57, B77, Pro2]

W2/1   Angels (1921, Curwen, 3 minutes)

6 muted trumpets. The first edition states that the work was composed for six muted trumpets, but that it may be played by "any six instruments of equal timbre." In the revised version [W2/2] for 4 trumpets and 2 muted trombones, Ruggles clarifies that the final instrumentation is as he desired it to be.

This work is dedicated to Charles L. Seeger.

[See: W2/2, W2/3, W14, D1, D15, D16, D17, B2, B11, B14, B21, B24, B25, B37, B38, B39, B58, B59, B64, B66, B67, B69, B75, B82, B116, B123, B125, B126, B131, B132, B134, B135, B137, B148, B151, B156, B163, B164, B168, B179, B186, B189, B193, B203, B206, B209, B218, Th1, Th3, Th7, Th8, C1a]

Premieres

W2/1a   1922 (27 April): New York, NY; Whitney Club. This performance, by string ensemble, was given as part of the last in a series of three lectures on modern music given by Ruggles.   This lecture was entitled "Technique and Phantasy in the Study of Composition."

[see: B82, B132, B148, B180, B218]

W2/1b 1922 (17 December): New York, NY; Klaw Theatre; First concert of the International Composers Guild season.

[see: B218]

Other Selected Performances

W2/1c 1925 (8 September): Venice; International Society of Contemporary Music Festival.

W2/1d 1933 (30 September): Saratoga Springs, NY; Second Yaddo Festival; Aeolian String Quartet with Messrs. Weiser and Stern.

[see: B49]

W2/2 **Angels** (1938, American Music Edition, 3 minutes)

4 muted C trumpets and 2 muted trombones, or for 4 violins and 2 cellos. The first edition [W2/1] states that the work was composed for six muted trumpets, but that it may be played by "any six instruments of equal timbre." In this revised version, Ruggles clarifies that the final instrumentation is as he desired it to be. This version is a minor third lower than the original and there is a slight extension of the middle section.

Angels was published in the 1943 series of New Music Edition along with *Evocations: Three Chants for Piano*.

This work is dedicated to Charles L. Seeger.

[See: W2/1, W2/3, W14, D1, D2, D12, B2, B14, B21, B24, B25, B37, B38, B39, B59, B64, B66, B75, B82, B100, B101, B115, B123, B125, B131, B134, B135, B151, B163, B164, B175, B179, B203, B206, B218, Th1, Th7, Th8, C1a]

Premiere

W2/2a 1939 (24 April): Miami, FL; Miami Senior High School Auditorium; ensemble of University of Miami students, conducted by the composer.

[see: B85, B218]

Other Selected Performances

W2/2b 1949 (27 February): New York, NY; Times Hall; concert given by the National Association of American Composers and Conductors; ensemble of Juilliard students, conducted by Lou Harrison.

[see: B132, B204, B205]

W2/2c 1961 (2 March): New York, NY; Museum of Modern Art; Composers' Showcase Concert sponsored by Charles Schwartz honoring Ruggles's 85th birthday; ensemble conducted by Robert Craft.

[see: W4/2e, W5i, W7h, B13, B68]

W2/2d 1968 (29 September): Bennington, VT; Mount Anthony Union High School; "Carl Ruggles Festival," a concert of the complete published works in conjunction with an exhibit of his paintings. Brass ensemble; Louis Calabro, conductor.

[see: W1b, W3b, W4/2f, W5j, W6d, W7i, W8c, B42,B57, B77, Pro2]

W2/3   Angels (1925, Curwen, 3 minutes)

This edition of *Angels* includes an organ transcription made by Lynnwood Farnam. Although Ruggles later withdrew his support of the string version of this work, he continued his support of the organ transcription.

The score is incribed "To Charles Louis Seeger, Jr."

[see: W2/1, W2/2]

W3   **Vox clamans in deserto** (1923, New Music Edition, 8 minutes)
   "Parting at Morning" - text: Robert Browning
   "Son of Mine" - text: Charles Henry Meltzer
   "A Clear Midnight" - text: Walt Whitman

mezzo-soprano and chamber orchestra {flute, oboe, clarinet, bassoon, horn, 2 trumpets, string sextet, and piano}

This work was available in manuscript only for many years. An engraved and corrected edition was published by Theodore Presser in 1977.

[See: W17, D1, B37, B38, B39, B64, B66, B69, B75, B89, B101, B131, B132, B134, B135, B151, B163, B168, B179, B189, B203, B206, B218, Th1, Th3, Th7, Th8, C1a]

Premiere

W3a   1924 (13 January): New York, NY; Vanderbilt Theatre; Second concert of the International Composers Guild season; Greta Torpadie, mezzo-soprano; conducted by Carlos Salzedo.

[see: B218]

Other Selected Performances

W3b   1968 (29 September): Bennington, VT; Mount Anthony Union High School; "Carl Ruggles Festival," a concert of the complete published works in conjunction with an exhibit of his paintings. Frank Baker, tenor; Bennington Chamber Ensemble; Lionel Nowak, conductor.

[see: W1b, W2/2d, W4/2f, W5j, W6d, W7i, W8c, B42, B57, B77, Pro2]

W4/1   **Men and Mountains** (1924, New Music Edition, 15 minutes)
    "Men: Rhapsodic Proclomation"
    "Lilacs" (7-part string orch)
    "Marching Mountains"

chamber orchestra {flute (doubling piccolo), oboe, English horn, clarinet, bassoon, 2 horns in F, 2 trumpets, trombone, 2 violins, 2 violas, 2 cellos, doublebass, and piano (a cymbal was added)}

Men and Mountains is dedicated to Eugene Schoen. The title was taken from William Blake.

[See: W4/2, W14, D7, B2, B11, B24, B36, B37, B38, B39, B64, B65, B66, B67, B69, B75, B100, B115, B123, B125, B127, B131, B132, B134, B135, B137, B148, B151, B163, B164, B168, B172, B179, B186, B187, B189, B193, B203, B206, B209, B218, Th1, Th3, Th7, Th8, C1a, C7]

Premiere

W4/1a   1924 (7 December): New York, NY; Aeolian Hall; First concert of the International Composers Guild season; conducted by Eugene Goosens.

[see: B163, B218]

Other Selected Performances

W4/1b 1931 (10 January): New York, NY; Town Hall; Chamber Orchestra of Boston; conducted by Nicolas Slonimsky. This concert featured the premiere of Charles Ives's *Three Places in New England.*

[see: B112, B127, B136, B141, B196, B212, B218]

W4/2 **Men and Mountains** (1936, revised 1941; New Music Edition; 15 minutes)
    "Men: Rhapsodic Proclamation"
    "Lilacs" (7-part string orch)
    "Marching Mountains"

full orchestra {3 flutes (3rd flute doubling piccolo), 3 oboes (3rd oboe doubling English horn), 3 clarinets (3rd clarinet doubling bass clarinet), 3 bassoons (3rd bassoon doubling contrabassoon), 4 horns, 3 trumpets, 3 trombones, 1 tuba, timpani, 3 percussionists, piano, and strings}

[See: W4/1, W14, D1, D2, D4, D11, D14, B2, B5, B15, B21, B24, B36, B37, B38, B39, B64, B65, B66, B75, B89, B100, B101, B115, B123, B125, B131, B132, B134, B135, B151, B156, B163, B164, B172, B176, B179, B190, B203, B206, B218, Th1, Th7, Th8, C1a]

Premieres

W4/2a 1931 (6 June): Paris; the first of a pair of concerts sponsored by the Pan American Association of Composers; conducted by Nicolas Slonimsky. This was the first performance of this work for full orchestra.

[see: W4/1, B132, B218, Pro3]

W4/2b 1936 (19 and 20 March): New York, NY: Carnegie Hall;
New York Philharmonic; conducted by Hans Lange. This
was the first performance of an expanded orchestration of
the first and third movements.

[see: B50]

Other Selected Performances

W4/2c 1950 (12 February): New York, NY; 12th Annual
American Music Festival; Manhattan School of Music
Orchestra; conducted by Harris Danziger. This concert was
broadcast by radio station WNYC.

[see: B218]

W4/2d 1958 (17, 18, and 19 October): New York, NY; New
York Philharmonic; conducted by Leonard Bernstein.

[see: B5, B56, B74, B76, Pro3]

W4/2e *Lilacs* only - 1961 (2 March): New York, NY; Museum of
Modern Art; Composers' Showcase Concert sponsored by
Charles Schwartz honoring Ruggles's 85th birthday;
ensemble conducted by Robert Craft.

[see: W2/2c, W5i, W7h, B13]

W4/2f 1968 (29 September): Bennington, VT; Mount Anthony
Union High School; "Carl Ruggles Festival," a concert of
the complete published works in conjunction with an
exhibit of his paintings. Vermont State Symphony
Orchestra; Alan Carter, conductor.

[see: W1b, W2/2d, W3b, W5j, W6d, W7i, W8c,
B42,B57, B77, Pro2]

W5   **Portals** (1925, transcribed for string orchestra in 1929, revised 1941 and 1952-53; American Music Editions; 6 minutes)

The score was initially for thirteen solo strings, which then was transribed for string-orchestra divided into 3 first violin parts, 2 second violin parts, 3 viola parts, 3 cello parts, and 2 double-bass parts.

The published score is a facsimile of the composers' manuscript. It is entitled "Portals Symphonic Composition for Full String Orchestra by Carl Ruggles," followed an inscription from Walt Whitman, "What are those of the known but to ascend and enter the unknown?"

This work is dedicated to Harriette Miller.

The manuscript of the title page is in the Bennington (VT) Museum.

[See: W19, D1, D4, B15, B21, B24, B37, B38, B39, B59, B64, B65, B66, B69, B75, B89, B100, B101, B115, B123, B125, B131, B132, B134, B135, B137, B141, B148, B151, B156, B163, B164, B168, B179, B187, B189, B203, B206, B207, B218, Th1, Th3, Th7, Th8, C1a, C11]

Premieres

for solo strings:

W5a   1926 (24 January): New York, NY; Aeolian Hall; as part of the International Composers Guild season; conducted by Eugene Goosens.

[see: B132, B218]

for string orchestra:

W5b   1929 (26 October): New York, NY, Carnegie Hall; the Conductorless Symphony Orchestra.

[see: B132, B218]

Other Selected Performances

W5c   1930: San Francisco; New Music Society Concert; conducted by Pedro Sanjuán.

[see: B218]

W5d   1931 (23 November): Madrid; conducted by Pedro Sanjuán.

[see: B218]

W5e   1931 (9 December): on an International Society for Contemporary Music concert; conducted by Ernst Ansermet.

[see: B218]

W5f   1932 (11 February): Vienna; Vienna Konzerthaus; Pan American Association of Composers concert; members of the Vienna Symphony Orchestra; conducted by Anton Webern.

W5g   1948 (13 May): New York, NY; Columbia May Festival; conducted by Frederick Fennell.

W5h   1953 (1 November): a CBS network radio braodcast concert; conducted by Stokowski.

W5i   1961 (2 March): New York, NY; Museum of Modern Art; Composers' Showcase Concert sponsored by Charles Schwartz honoring Ruggles's 85th birthday; ensemble conducted by Robert Craft.

[see: W2/2c, W4/2e, W7h, B13, B68]

W5j   1968 (29 September): Bennington, VT; Mount Anthony Union High School; "Carl Ruggles Festival," a concert of the complete published works in conjunction with an exhibit of his paintings. Northeastern New York Philharmonia; Edgar Curtis, music director; Anthony Pezzano, conducting.

[see: W1b, W2/2d, W3b, W4/2f, W5j, W6d, W7i, W8c, B42,B57, B77, Pro2]

W6   **Sun-Treader** (1931, New Music Edition, 15 minutes)

full orchestra {2 piccolos, 3 flutes, 3 oboes, 2 English horns, clarinet in Eb, 3 clarinets in C, bass clarinet, 3 bassoons, contrabassoon, six horns in F, 5 trumpets in C, 3 trombones, tenor tuba in C, bass tuba, timpani, 2 cymbals (high and low), 2 harps, 18-20 first violins, 18-20, second violins, 12-14 violas, 10-12 cellos, and 8-10 double basses}

The title is taken from Robert Browning's description of Shelley: "Sun-treader, light and life be thine forever." This title was first used for the third movement of the incomplete *Men and Angels*.

[See: D1, D3, D5, D8, B2, B4, B7, B8, B9, B20, B21, B23, B24, B28, B37, B38, B39, B59, B65, B66, B69, B75, B81, B89, B100, B101, B115, B123, B125, B127, B131, B132, B134, B135, B137, B148, B151, B163, B168, B177, B179, B189, B203, B206, B209, B218, Th1, Th3, Th6, Th7, Th8, Th9, C1a]

Premieres

W6a   1932 (25 February): Paris; Salle Playel; Orchestra Symphonique de Paris; conducted by Nicolas Slonimsky. Slonimsky led further performances shortly afterward in Berlin and Prague.

[see: B7, B99, B132, B163, B212, B218]

W6b   1966 (24 January): Portland, Maine; Portland City Hall Auditorium; given in conjunction with the festivsal of Ruggles's music on the Bowdoin College Biennial Institute; Boston Symphony Orchestra conducted by Jean Martinon. American Premiere.

[see: B7, B16, B40, B48, B73, B218, Pro1]

Other Selected Performances

W6c   1936 (22 April): Barcelona, Spain: 14th Festival of the International Society for Contemporary Music; Philharmonic Orchestra of Madrid; conducted by Pedro Sanjuán. This concert was broadcast live on the radio to the United States by WABC.

[see: B7, B218]

W6d   1968 (29 September): Bennington, VT; Mount Anthony Union High School; "Carl Ruggles Festival," a concert of the complete published works in conjunction with an exhibit of his paintings. Bennington Community Orchestra, Berkshire Symphony Orchestra, Northeastern New York Philharmonia, and Vermont State Symphony; Henry Brant, conductor.
[see: W1b, W2/2d, W3b, W4/2f, W5j, W6d, W7i, W8c, B7, B42, B57, B77, Pro2]

W7   **Evocations: Four Chants for Piano** (1937-43, revised 1954; New Music Edition, 11 minutes)

> Largo (1937)
> Andante con Fantasia (1941)
> Moderato Appassionato (1943)
> Adagio Sostenuto (1940)

All but the third movement were published in the 1943 series of New Music Edition along with *Angels*, under the title, *Evocations: Three Chants for Piano*. For this publication they were edited by John Kirkpatrick. The revised score, including the Moderato movement, was published in 1954. The revisions were made in preparation for the first recording of the work [D4]. Ruggles also indicated occasional desire that the Moderato and Adagio movements be reversed.

The works are dedicated to Harriette Miller, John Kirkpatrick, Charlotte Ruggles, and Charles Ives respectively.

[See: W15, W21, D1, D4, D9, D13, D18, D19, D20, B15, B18, B20, B21, B22, B25, B29, B37, B38, B39, B41, B66, B75, B94, B100, B125, B131, B132, B134, B135, B147, B151, B163, B164, B168, B172, B179, B193, B203, B206, B218, Th1, Th3, Th4, Th7, Th8, C1a, C3]

Premieres

W7a   1940 (18 November): Greenwich, CT; private recital; John Kirkpatrick, piano [two pieces].

[see: B218]

W7b   1941 (31 January): Detroit, MI; Detroit Institute of Arts in a concert sponsored by Pro Musica in conjunction with a show of Ruggles's paintings and drawings; John Kirkpatrick, piano [two pieces].

[see: B62, B218]

W7c   1942 (14 January): New York, NY; Town Hall;   John Kirkpatrick, piano [three pieces].

Other Selected Performances

W7d   1948 (17 February): New York, NY; T. L. Kaufman Auditorium; William Masselos, piano.

W7e   1949 (1 April): Bennington, VT; Bennington College; Julian DeGray, piano.

W7f   1950 (11 February): New York, NY; International Society for Contemporary Music Concert; Irene Rosenberg, piano.

W7g   1952 (5 July): Arlington, VT; Southern Vermont Art Center in conjunction with the opening of a one-man show of Ruggles's paintings; John Kirkpatrick, piano.

W7h   1961 (2 March): New York, NY; Museum of Modern Art; Composers' Showcase Concert sponsored by Charles Schwartz honoring Ruggles's 85th birthday; Lionel Nowak, piano.

[see: W2/2c, W4/2e, W5i, B13, B68]

W7i   1968 (29 September): Bennington, VT; Mount Anthony Union High School; "Carl Ruggles Festival," a concert of the complete published works in conjunction with an exhibit of his paintings. Julian DeGray, piano.

[see: W1b, W2/2d, W3b, W4/2f, W5j, W6d, W7i, W8c, B42,B57, B77, Pro2]

W8   **Organum** (1944-47, New Music Edition, 8 minutes)

orchestra {piccolo, 2 flutes, 2 oboes, English horn, Eb clarinet, 3 <u>clarinets in C</u>, bass clarinet, 2 bassoons, contrabassoon, 4 horns, 3 trumpets, 3 trombones, tuba, piano, timpani, cymbal, and strings}

[See: W16, D1, D6, D10, B8, B12, B16, B20, B37, B38, B39, B59, B66, B75, B94, B100, B101, B115, B123, B125, B131, B132, B134, B135, B151, B163, B164, B168, B174, B179, B203, B206, B218, Th1, Th7, Th8, C1a]

Premiere

W8a   1949 (24 and 25 November): New York, NY; Carnegie Hall; New York Philharmonic; conducted by Leopold Stokowski. A private recording was made of the second performance.

[see: B12, B59, B114, B132, B195, B218, Pro3]

Other Selected Performances

W8b   1950 (8 and 9 March); Cleveland Orchestra; conducted by George Szell.

W8c   1968 (29 September): Bennington, VT; Mount Anthony Union High School; "Carl Ruggles Festival," a concert of the complete published works in conjunction with an exhibit of his paintings. Berkshire Symphony Orchestra; Julius Hegyi, conductor.

[see: W1b, W2/2d, W3b, W4/2f, W5j, W6d, W7i, W8c, B42,B57, B77, Pro2]

W9   **The Sunken Bell** (c.1912-23, unpublished)

This opera, libretto by Charles H. Meltzer from the play *Die versunkene Glocke* by Gerhart Hauptmann, was destroyed except for sketches.

[see: B5, B6, B7, B10, B25, B39, B66, B83, B86, B123, B132, B134, B135, B138, B151, B159, B203, B206, B218, Th5, M2, C1a]

W10   **Mood** (c. 1918, unpublished)

violin and piano

[see: B218, C1a]

W10a   1976 (19 January): New Haven, CT; Sprague Hall at Yale University; This premiere was based upon a construction made by John Kirkpatrick from five sketches. Dan Stepner, violin; and John Kirkpatrick, piano.

[see: B46]

W11   **Symphonia Dialecta**, "Affirmations for Orchestra" (1923, unpublished)

orchestra (unfinished)

[see: B53, B218, C1a]

W12   **Polyphonic Composition** (1940, unpublished)

3 pianos

[see: W66, B149, B218, C1a]

W13   **Exaltation** (1958, unpublished)

Hymn for Congregation in Unison with organ

[See: D1, B38, B125, B218, C1a]

Premiere

W13a   1966 (11 June): Brunswick, ME; Bowdoin College Gymnasium; performed by the Bowdoin College Choir with a brass choir arranged by Elliott Schwartz and text written by the college poet, Louis Coxe. This performance was given as part of the college's commencement program which included bestowing an honorary doctorate upon Ruggles.

[see: B48]

W14   **Men and Angels** (1921, unpublished)

orchestra {piccolo, 3 flutes, 2 oboes, English horn, 2 clarinets, bass clarinet, 3 bassoons, contrabassoon, 6 horns, 3 trumpets, 3 trombones, tuba, timpani, cymbal, and strings} Marilyn Zifrin notes that there was space allocated for two harps, but no music placed there.[1]

Material from this composition was reworked into *Angels* and *Men and Mountains*. The third movement, which is the model of the first movement of *Men and Mountains*, is entitled "Suntreader," but is not musically linked to Ruggles's completed work of the same title.

[See: W2/1, W2/2, W4/1, W4/2, D1, B38, B64, B82, B89, B116, B126, B148, B163, B186, B187, B218, C1a]

---

[1] Zifrin, Marilyn: *Carl Ruggles: Composer, Painter, and Storyteller*. Urbana, University of Illinois Press, 1994.

W15   Evocations (1942-45, unpublished)

orchestra

This is an orchestral arrangement of *Evocations* for piano.

[See: W7, W21, D1, B29, B38, B89, B99, B101, B125, B218, C1a]

W15a   1971 (2 February): New York, NY; Carnegie Hall; a concert given by the National Orchestra Association under John Perras. This was his debut as a conductor.

[see: B29]

W16   Organum (1946-47, unpublished)

This is a two-piano arrangement of the orchestral work.

[see: W8, B218, C1a]

W16a   1947 (20 April): New York, NY; New School for Social Research; New Music Society concert; Maro Ajemian and William Masselos, pianists.

[see: B94]

W17   Sea Pattern (unpublished)

Incomplete movement for *Vox clamans in deserto*
Text: Walt Whitman, "As if a Phantom Caress'd Me"

[See: W3, B218, C1a]

W18   Windy Nights (unpublished)

sketch
Text: Robert Louis Stevenson

[see: B218, C1a]

W19   **Portals** (incomplete movements - unpublished)

> Scherzo
> Finale
> a coda for the first movement
> Largo espressivo

string orchestra

[See: W5, B218, C1a]

W20   **Parvum organum** (unpublished)

piano

[see: B218, C1a]

W21   **Evocation No.5** (unpublished)

5th movement for Evocations

[See: W7, W15, B29, B218, C1a]

W22   **Flower Pieces** (unpublished)

> "Wake-robin"
> "Delphinium"
> "White Violets"

piano

[see: B213, B218, C1a]

W23   **opus 1** (1899, C. W. Thompson and Co.)

withdrawn by the composer

"How Can I be Blythe and Glad"
"At Sea"
"Maiden with Thy Mouth of Roses"

voice and piano

[see: B84, B218, C1a]

W24   Thy Presence Ever Near Me (1901, Arthur P. Schmidt)

withdrawn by the composer

voice and piano

[see: B84, B218, C1a]

W25   Valse de Concert (unpublished)

[see: B218, C1a]

DISCOGRAPHY

D1   **Columbia M2-34591**, 33 rpm LP, 2 discs, released: 1980

Buffalo Philharmonic, members of Speculum Musicae, Gregg Smith Singers - Michael Tilson Thomas, conductor; Brass Ensemble - Gerard Schwartz, leader; Judith Blegen, soprano; John Kirkpatrick, piano; Beverly Morgan, voice; Leonard Raver, organ.

Works included: *Toys*, recorded: May 1978; *Angels* (1921 version) recorded: March 1977; *Angels* (1938 version), recorded: March 1977; *Vox Clamans in Deserto* recorded: May 1978; *Men and Mountains* (full-orchestra version), recorded: November 1975; *Portals*, recorded: May 1976; *Sun-Treader*, recorded: November 1975; *Evocations*, recorded: October 1977; *Organum*, recorded: May 1976; *Exaltation*, recorded: March 1977; *Men and Angels*, recorded: May 1976; *Evocations* (orchestral version), recorded: November 1975

[See: W1, W2/1, W2/2, W3, W4/2, W5, W6, W7, W8, W13, W14, W15, B2, B29, B38, B106, B125, B169]

D2   **Turnabout/Vox TV-S 34398**, 33 rpm LP, released: 1971

Buffalo Philharmonic - Lucas Foss, conductor

Works included: *Angels* (1938 version), *Men and Mountains* (full-orchestra version)

[See: W2/2, W4/2, B169]

D3   **Deutsche Grammophon 2530.048**, 33 rpm LP, released: 1970; also released as Deutsche Grammophon 2563.039 in set 2721.020, 33 rpm LP's; rereleased as Deutsche Grammophon (20th Century Classics) 429860-2, compact disc [ADD], 1991

Boston Symphony Orchestra - Michael Tilson Thomas

Works included: *Sun-Treader*, recorded: 24 March 1970; also Charles Ives - *Three Places in New England*.

[See: W6, B9, B169]

D4   **Columbia ML-4986**, 33 rpm LP, released: 1955, deleted: 1968; rereleased as
Columbia CML-4986: 1968, deleted: 1974; released as AML-4986: 1974

Julliard String Orchestra - Frederik Prausnitz, conductor; John Kirkpatrick, piano

Works included: *Men and Mountains* (2nd movement only), recorded: <u>13 May 1954;</u> *Portals*, recorded: 2 March 1955; *Evocations*, recorded: 13 May 1954

[See: W4/2, W5, W7, B4, B15, B66, B105, B169]

D5   **International Contemporary Exchange-American Anthology**

Works included: *Sun-Treader*

[See: W6, B169]

D6   **Leopold Stokowski conducting on Carnegie Hall in-house recording**

Works included: *Organum*

[See: W8, B169, C1, C9]

D7   **New Music Quarterly Recording 1013**, 78 rpm records, 6 discs, released: 1934; W4 rereleased as: Orion ORD-7150/ORS-7150, 33 rpm LP: 1971

Pan-American Chamber Orchestra - Charles Lichter, conductor; Henry Brant, piano; Judith Litante, soprano

Works included: *Toys*; *Men and Mountains* (2nd movement only), recorded: 16 May 1934

[See: W1, W4/1, B132, B158, B163, B169, C1]

D8   **Columbia MS-6801/MS-6801**, 33 rpm LP, released: 1966, deleted: 1971

Columbia Symphony Orchestra - Zoltan Rozsnyai, conductor

Works included: *Sun-Treader*, recorded: 8 and 9 March 1965; Also: Robert Helps - *Symphony No. 1*

[See: W6, B4, B8, B40, B66, B81, B169]

D9   **Vox SVBX 5303**, 33 rpm LP, 3 discs, released: 1977

Roger Shields, piano

Works included: *Evocations*, recorded: 1976

[See: W7, B169]

D10   **CRI SD-127**, 33 rpm LP, released: 1960

Japan Philharmonic Symphony Orchestra - Akeo Watanabe

Works included: *Organum*

[See: W8, B66, B169]

D11   **CRI S-254**, 33 rpm LP, released: 1970

Polish National Radio Orchestra - William Strickland

Works included: *Men and Mountains* (full-orchestra version), recorded: 1968

[See: W4/2, B169]

D12   **Lehigh RINC-1103**, 33 rpm LP, released: 1968, deleted: 1976

Lehigh University Instrumental Ensemble - Jonathan Elkus, conductor

Works included: *Angels* (1938 version), recorded: 30 April 1960

[See: W2/2, B66, B169]

D13   **Desto DC-6445-47**, 33 rpm LP, 3 discs, released: 1975

Alan Mandel, piano

Works included: *Evocations*

[See: W7, B41, B106, B169]

D14   **Hammar SD-150**, 33 rpm LP

New Hampshire Music Festival Orchestra - Thomas Nee, conductor

Works included: *Men and Mountains* (chamber-orchestra version), recorded: 14 July 1976

[See: W4/2, B169]

D15   **Teldec 2292-46442-2**, compact disc [DDD], 2 discs, released: 1991

"Modern Times With London Brass" — London Brass

Works included: *Angels* (1921 version)

[See: W2/1]

D16   **Hyperion CDA 66517**, compact disc

London Gabrieli Brass Ensemble

Works included: *Angels* (1921 version)

[See: W2/1]

D17   **Summit DCD 122**, compact disc [DDD]

Ensemble 21 - Arthur Weisberg, conductor

Works included: *Angels* (1921 version)

[See: W2/1]

D18   **Centaur CRC 2082**, compact disc [DDD], released: 1990

A. Stokman, piano

Works included: *Evocations* (original version)

[See: W7]

D19   New World 80402-2, compact disc [DDD]

Michael Boriskin, piano

Works included: *Evocations* (revised version)

[See: W7]

D20   Music and Arts Programs of America CD757, compact disc [DDD]

J. Jensen, piano

Works included: *Evocations* (revised version)

[See: W7]

RUGGLES AS AUTHOR

A 1   *The Watertown Tribune* **(MA), 27 November 1902 to 6 November 1903.**

Ruggles served as the music critic for this newspaper. Of a total of twenty-eight articles: eighteen are concert reviews, and ten are essays on various musical subjects. These reviews also appeared in *The Belmont Tribune* the following day.

N.B. After 3 April 1903 it became *The Watertown Tribune-Enterprise.*

[see: A2, B84]

A 2   *The Belmont Tribune* **(MA), 28 November 1902 to 7 November 1903.**

These music reviews were reprinted from *The Watertown Tribune* of the previous day.

[see: A1, B84]

GENERAL BIBLIOGRAPHY

JOURNAL AND NEWSPAPER ARTICLES

B 1   **Affelder, Paul:** *Symphony News*: **"Carl Ruggles (1876-1971)," volume 22, number 6 (1971), 16.**

This is a short essay on Ruggles and his compositional style which substitutes for an obituary. The author discusses the small output of the composer and his limited representation in concerts as a response to his compositional method and individual style.

B 2   **Babcock, David: "Carl Ruggles: Two Early Works and** *Sun-Treader*,**"** *Tempo* **135 (December 1980), 3.**

This article begins as an introduction to the composer and his works, all of which are discussed briefly. Following this, there are analyses of *Angels*, *Men and Mountains*, and *Sun-Treader*. This study is filled with musical examples. Babcock suggests that Ruggles's technique of avoiding pitch repetition is not so much to escape tonality, but rather an attempt to emulate Bach's melodic invention within the context of the avant-garde. He emphasizes that upon repeated listening a clear sense of order becomes apparent. Babcock also describes *Sun-Treader* as being in Sonata-Allegro form for which he provides a clear analysis. He also demonstrates that Ruggles's pitch use is an extension of tonal principles and that this is the central factor controlling his shaping of larger formal structures.

[See: W2, W4, W6, D1]

B 3   **"Berichte aus Amerika II. Die beiden wirkliche Amerikaner: Ives und Ruggles," *Melos*, volume 9, number 10 (October 1930).**

This is an introduction to European readers of the musical procedures and works of Ives and Ruggles with allusions drawn between Ruggles and the techniques of the Schoenberg—Webern—Berg circle. It is written in German.

B 4   **Boretz, Benjamin: "Music," *The Nation* 202 (7 March 1966), 278-80.**

This article is an evaluation of all Ruggles's compositions against the backdrop of his peers, whom Boretz states are experiencing a renaissance upon American college campuses as university composers and their students seek to find their roots. The author circuitously praises and berates the music of Ruggles and his contemporaries. The essay seems to be prompted by the Carl Ruggles Festival at Bowdoin College [for which Boretz served in a panel discussion] and the recent release of the first recording of *Sun-Treader*.

[see: W6, D4, D8]

B 5   **Briggs, John: "Crusty Composer," *New York Times* (12 October 1958), section 2, p. 11:8.**

This is an announcement of an upcoming concert featuring works of three "older American" composers: Ruggles, John Becker, and Wallingford Riegger, by the New York Philharmonic under Leonard Bernstein. *Men and Mountains* was presented on this program.

[see: W4/2, W4/2d, W9]

B 6   *Central Opera.* **"Obituary," 14 (Summer 1972), 18.**

Although a mere three-sentence notice in the necrology section, it includes a unique explanation for the abandonment of Ruggles's opera: "... *The Sunken Bell* had been under consideration by the Metropolitan Opera for production; however, it came to naught when the company refused to have a special bell cast for the occasion."

[see: W9, B86]

B 7   **Christiansen, Beth: *"Sun-Treader*, Reluctant Dawn, Bringing Carl Ruggles's Masterpiece to America,"** *American Music***, 9:3 (1991).**

Ms. Christiansen presents a brief biography of the composer followed by a detailed account of the various performances of *Sun-Treader*, and the production of the *New Music Edition* score, including the financial support from Ives to guarantee the first performance and to bring it into print. Additionally, she discusses Ruggles's friendship with Thomas Hart Benton, whose painting of Ruggles, entitled *Sun-Treader*, appears on the journal's cover.

[see: W6, W6a, W6b W6c, W6d, W9]

B 8   **Cohn, Arthur: "Now That Other American Giant: Carl Ruggles,"** *American Record Guide* **32 (March 1966).**

This is a review of the first recording of *Sun-Treader*. The author mentions a number of personal reflections about his contact with Ruggles's music and a correspondence he had with the composer regarding his craft. Short notice is also given to Robert Helps's *Symphony No. 1*. Cohn greets

Sun-Treader with delight, and the Helps work with disinterest; however, he commends the quality of performance for both.

[see: W6, D8]

B9 _____. **"Playing and Conducting That Simply Could Not Be Bettered,"** *American Record Guide* **volume 37 (November 1970), 148-51.**

This is a review of Michael Tilson Thomas's first recording which he made as the associate conductor of the Boston Symphony Orchestra. It contains Ives's *Three Places in New England* and Ruggles's *Sun-Treader*. The review is enthusiastically supportive of both works and the quality and depth of the performances.

[see: W6, D3]

B10 **Cowell, Henry: "Three Native Composers,"** *New Freeman* **1 (3 May 1930).**

In this essay Cowell attacks the eurocentrism of American musical tastes: "Our American composers who originate something new and of this soil (either in materials or style) therefore not only do not become famous for it, but their chances of production are actually more limited than if they were to write half-baked rehashes of Europe's mildest talents." He then describes the technical and æsthetic developments of Ives, Ruggles, and Roy Harris, citing them as three typical cases of American originality in music. In his description of Ruggles, Cowell suggests that it was in the period of composition for *The Sunken Bell* that Ruggles developed his mature polyphonic method.

[see: W9]

B11 _____: **"Carl Ruggles,"** *The Carmelite* **3 (August 1930).**

This article is an elaboration upon the section on Ruggles in "Three Native Composers," in the *New Freeman* 1. It contains biographical information and an introduction to the works.

[see: W2/1, W4/1]

B12   _____: "Organum," in "Current Chronicle," *Musical Quarterly*, volume 36, number 2 (April 1950), 272-4.

This is a review of the premiere of *Organum* by the New York Philharmonic under Leopold Stokowski. Cowell lauds the work and uses his review as an opportunity to explain the foundation of Ruggles's technique. Cowell also states that the work received "real popular success," noting how this is a significant change from Ruggles's New York premieres in the 1920s.

[See: W8, W8a]

B13   Diether, Jack: "Composer's Showcase," *Musical America* 81 (May 1961), 52.

This is a brief review of the second Composers' Showcase Concert presented by Charles Schwartz at the Museum of Modern Art in New York. This program was given in honor of Ruggles's eighty-fifth birthday, featuring works by the honoree: *Lilacs*, *Angels*, *Portals*, and *Evocations*; and songs by Charles Ives.

N.B. Lionel Nowak's name is misspelled.

[See: W2/2c, W4/2e, W5i, W7h]

B14   Dombek, Stephen: "A Study of Harmonic Interrelationships and Sonority Types in Carl Ruggles's *Angels*," *Indiana Theory Review*, 4:1 (1980), 29.

This study of *Angels* examines differences in previous analyses of the same work by Harman, Ostander, and Zifrin. The author cites many sources which describe *Angels* as a the final transitional step toward Ruggles's method of non-repetition of pitches, yet he appears surprised by the presence of tonal elements within the work. Of particular interest are two original analyses of *Angels*: the first applies Schenkerian concepts of abstraction and distillation complete with traditional Schenkerian graphing procedures, the second is a pitch-class vector analysis of each measure showing the careful arrangement of dissonances throughout the composition. Lastly, Dombek determines that much of the secundal language of the piece conceals sets of triadic structures juxtaposed in parallel minor seconds, thereby cleverly conjoining traditional and modern techniques into one unique pitch vocabulary.

[See: W2/1, W2/2, B24, B82]

B15   Ellsworth, Roy: "Americans on Microgroove,"
***HiFi* 6 (August 1956), 60-66.**

Ellsworth's article is a survey of American music available at that time on LP recordings. The descriptions are presented in a free-flowing narrative of the various styles and trends in American concert music to that date rather than in an ordered catalogue-like form. In fact, Ruggles is mentioned in three places, though examined in only one. There is a brief description of Columbia ML-4986, listed in the article as ML-4968.

[see: W4/2, W5, W7, D4]

B16   Ericson, Raymond: "Ruggles—90 Years Young," ***New York Times* (16 January 1966), section 2, 27-28.**

A double-angled article; it announces the Carl Ruggles Festival to be held at Bowdoin College, including a brief discussion of the composer's career and compositional style; and it reviews the premiere recording of *Sun-Treader*.

[see: W6b, D8]

B17   *Facts on File*: "Dies (Age 95)," 31 (24 October 1971), 1039, column 2.

Ruggles's death is acknowledged with a three-sentence description of his career.

B18   Fischer, Fred: "Contemporary American Style: Showing How Three Representative Composers Use the 'Row'," *Clavier*, volume 14, number 4 (1975), 34-37.

Fischer analyzes *Evocations* as if it were a serial composition. While admitting that the work does not conform to traditional serial procedures, he suggests that Ruggles uses three- and four-note motivic germs which are transposed, mutated, and intertwined to create a unique pitch fabric. These procedures are not effectively connected with the other works discussed in the article.

[see: W7]

B19   Fleming, Shirley: "Carl Ruggles Festival; Brunswick Report," *HiFi* 16 (April 1966), 158.

This is a review of the Carl Ruggles Festival sponsored by Bowdoin College. It is an article sympathetic to the composer, and to some extent it is even defensive: "...the entire affair might prompt some soul-searching as to the way in which this country manages to ignore the work of its more original creative minds." Fleming evaluates the various performances and lectures of the festival upholding an evident opinion that the expressivity of the music as performed out-values its technical details as presented by musicological constituency.

B20   **Gilbert, Steven E.: "Carl Ruggles (1876-1971): An Appreciation,"** *Perspectives in New Music,* **volume 11, number 1 (Fall-Winter 1972), 224-32.**

This essay begins by comparing and contrasting Ruggles to his friend Ives. Gilbert suggests that Ruggles's music is consistently more abstract and in a sense more introverted. He then discusses Ruggles's role in the the Pan-American Association of Composers, pointing out the generally experimental nature of its member composers. The remainder of the article is a brief overview of the compositional procedures used in Ruggles's music with a focus upon his methods of pitch organization.

[see: W6, W7, W8]

B21   **_____: " 'The Ultra-Modern Idiom': A Survey of** *New Music*,**"** *Perspectives in New Music,* **volume 12, numbers 1-2 (Fall-Winter 1973 / Spring-Summer 1974), 282-314.**

This is an overview of the works and composers represented by the serial, *New Music Edition*, and its companion series of recordings, *New Music Quarterly Recordings*. Gilbert suggests that the composers presented in Cowell's publication were generally the members of the Pan-American Association of Composers which had far less public exposure and commercial appeal than those affiliated with the League of Composers, and that the publication and the composers had a symbiotic relationship. He surveys the various compositional processes evident in this repertoire, especially the various atonal procedures which developed alongside those of the Second Viennese School. Ruggles is mentioned as a principal composer in the series and for his influence upon works by Dane Rudhyar, Merton Brown, John Becker, and Lou Harrison.

[see: W2/1,W2/2, W4/2, W5, W6,W7]

B22   _____: **"The 'Twelve-Tone System' of Carl Ruggles: a Study of the *Evocations for Piano,"* *Journal of Music Theory*, 14 (1970), 68-91.**

Gilbert begins his article by indicating that although he is aware of the revised edition of 1956, it was "unavailable" to him, and therefore his analysis is based upon the first published editions. In a narrative format, he goes through the analytical process and changes his course throughout, first stating that *Evocation No. 2* is a twelve-tone work, then that it is not, and finally that it is in a sense. The principal analytical device which he uses is Allen Forte's pitch-class set method. Ultimately, after thorough dissection, Gilbert concludes that Ruggles's work is freely atonal and unique in its avoidance of a systematic treatment of intervals while maintaining a consistent emphasis upon dissonant secundal harmonies, a conclusion which had been stated by Ruggles and his associates numerous times before.

[see: W7]

B23   _____: **"Carl   Ruggles   and   Total Chromaticism,"** *Yearbook for Inter-American Musical Research*, **7 (1971), 43.**

In this article, first presented as a paper at the 1970 Annual Meeting of the American Musicological Society in Toronto, Gilbert begins with a comparison of the lives and works Ives and Ruggles and proceeds to analyze the pitch procedures used by the latter as evidenced in *Sun-Treader*. Using pitch-class set analysis, he demonstrates the avoidance of pitch repetition, and notes that the melodic material breaks neatly into similar trichords. Gilbert suggests that the regularity of these trichord sets, and Ruggles's reputation for being painstakingly methodical, indicate that this organization is much more intentional than the composer was inclined to admit.

[See: W6]

B24   Harman, Dave R.: "The Musical Language of Carl Ruggles (1876-1971)," *American Music Teacher*, volume 25, number 5 (1976), 25-27.

This article is a general introduction to the composer and his techniques. Harman examines the compositional elements of melody, harmony, rhythm, counterpoint, orchestration, and form in Ruggles's music citing specific works for each element. He concludes that the value of Ruggles's contribution to music will remain unknown until more performances have taken place, and that we have distanced ourselves from the modern era.

[See: W2, W4, W5, W6, B14, B82]

B25   Harrison, Lou: *About Carl Ruggles*. A pamphlet: Yonkers, New York: Alicat Bookshop, 1946; mostly reprinted in *The Score*, 12 (1955), 15.

Harrison draws a comparison between Ruggles and Handel, explaining that each composer had a distinctive sound and an exceptionally intuitive sense of sonority and texture. He discusses the development of Ruggles's polyphonic techniques, stating that his work on *The Sunken Bell* functioned as an apprenticeship through which his compositional method took shape, and he suggests that it is a logical continuation of the contrapuntal explorations of Bach and Handel. Harrison then discusses *Evocations* in detail, including the pervasive use of the "after-note" technique. He draws direct comparison between these piano pieces and Schoenberg's opus 11. Harrison states that of the composers of the modern era, Ruggles is the most consistent in his procedures and musical language.

[See: W2, W7, W9, B27, B129]

B26   _____: "Ruggles, Ives, Varèse," *View*, volume 5, number 4 (November 1945) 11.

This article champions "America's three greatest living composers." Harrison describes the role of each in the fabric of American artistic culture and questions the dearth of performances of their music: "... it is one of the lamentations of the young that they are not hearing it now. In fact the young are feeling cheated in this whole matter. And why should they not? It is quite possible to see Betty Grable more frequently than to hear the best of this century's Usonian music."

[see: B129]

B27   _____: "Carl Ruggles," *The Score*, number 12 (June 1955).

This is a reprint of the 1946 article listed above: *About Carl Ruggles*, as published in pamphlet form by the Alicat Bookshop.

[see: B25, B129]

B28   Harvey, J. H.: "Minneapolis: Ruggles Festival." *HiFi/Musical America* 24 (August 1974), 30-31.

This is a description of a festival held in Minneapolis and St. Paul from March through June of 1974 honoring Ruggles. The festival was the off-shoot of research conducted by Nina Archabal for her dissertation on the composer/painter. The festival included concerts, an art exhibit, and lectures on Ruggles as composer and visual artist.

[see: W6, Th1]

B29   Henahan, Donal: " 'Evocations' by Ruggles" *New York Times* (4 February 1971), 28:3.

This is a review of the premiere of *Evocations* in orchestrated form, which was given by the National Orchestral Association under John Perras on 2 February.

The concert was Perras's debut as a conductor. Henahan is lukewarm about the performance, suggesting that the level of the student performers which constitute this orchestra is not up to what is required for a meaningful reading.

[see: W7, W15, W15a, W21, D1]

B30   _____: "Carl Ruggles, Composer, Is Dead at 95"** *New York Times* **(26 October 1971), 45:2.**

This substantial obituary includes a biographical summary of the composer and an interview with John Kirkpatrick regarding the condition and future of Ruggles's estate.

[see: C1a]

B31   *HiFi/Musical America.* **"Obituary," 22 (February 1972),** *MA* **2.**

This is a single sentence announcement of the composer's death as part of the "Here and There" page.

B32   *Independent, The.*   **Winona, MN, 1907-18.**

[see: B61, Th10, C7]

Carl and Charlotte Ruggles are mentioned briefly in the following issues of this local newspaper. Most of the entries are social pages and concert announcements for the Winona Orchestra.

1907: Feb: 1, p.5; 24, p. 3; 26, p.5; Mar: 15, p. 5; 19, p. 3; 20, p. 5; 21, p.8; 24, p. 5; 27, p. 5; 28, p. 5; Apr: 5, p. 8; 6, p. 8; 17, p.5; May: 11, p.5; 22, p. 2; 28, p. 2; June: 2, p. 8; 14, p. 3; Aug: 31, p.6; Sept: 11, p. 3; 15, p. 8; 17, p. 8; 21, p. 6; 22, p. 4; Oct: 6, p.3 and 8; 20, p. 8; 27, p. 6; 31, p. 6; Nov: 1, p. 6; 3, p. 4; 8, p. 3; 21, p. 6; Dec: 1, p. 6; 8, p. 8; 14, p. 3; 15, p.8; 22, p. 6.

1908: Jan: 5, p. 8; 8, p.6; 12, p. 8; 19, p. 8; 26, p. 8; 30, p. 6; 31, p. 6; Feb: 8, p. 3; 9, p. 8; 14, p. 6; 16, p. 8; 18, p. 5; 23, p. 3; Mar: 4, p. 3; 5, p. 6; 7, p. 2; 8, p. 2 and 7; 15 p. 6; 22, p. 8; 24, p. 6; 29, p. 8; Apr: 5, p. 5 and 6; 7, p.6; 9, p. 8, 11, p. 3; 12, p. 2 and 3; 19, p.2; 23, p. 6; 25, p.6 ; 26, p. 2 and 3; 28, p. 6; 29, p. 5 and 6; 30, p. 3 and 6; May: 1, p. 2; 3, p. 5; 10, p.5; 22, p. 8; 23, p. 6; 24, p. 8; 27, p. 8; 28, p. 6; June: 14, p. 4; Jul: 19, p. 8; Sept: 4, p. 3; 10, p. 5; 19, p. 6; 27, p. 5; Oct: 1, p. 5; 3, p. 8; 4, p. 6; 8, p. 6; 20, p. 3; Nov: 7, p. 5; 8, p. 3 and 5; 10, p. 6; 24, p. 6; 25, p. 3; 29, p. 10; Dec: 2, p. 6; 12, p. 8; 20, p. 4.

1909: Jan: 14, p. 5; 17, p. 7; 19, p. 8; 20, p. 6 and 8; 21, p. 6; 24, p. 6; 27, p. 8; 30, p. 5; 31, p. 5; Feb: 3, p. 6; 4, p. 5; 5, p. 4; 7, p. 6; 10, p. 3; 12, p. 8; 16, p. 3; 25, p. 6; 27, p. 8; Mar: 4, p. 3 and 6; 5, p. 3; 6, p. 6; 12, p. 6;19, p. 3; 20, p. 6; 24, p. 6; 25, p. 8; 26, p. 6; 27, p. 6; Apr: 4, p. 3; 11, p. 2; 21, p. 9; 28, p. 3 and 6; 29, p. 6; 30, p. 6; May: 1, p. 6; 28, p. 6; June: 20,p. 5; Sept: 19, p. 8; 23, p. 6; 25, p. 8; Oct: 2, p. 6; 3, p. 3; 5, p. 3; 17, p. 2; 24, p. 8; 30, p. 4; 31, p. 9; Nov: 4, p. 5; 4, p. 3; 7, p. 7; 17, p. 3; 21, p. 2; 28, p. 6; Dec: 1, p. 6; 2, p. 8; 3, p. 6 and 8; 4, p. 2; 14, p. 6; 19, p. 8.

1910: Jan: 1, p. 5; 9, p. 8; 11, p. 6; 16, p. 6; 18, p. 6; 19, p. 6; 25, p. 8; 30, p. 4 and 6; Feb: 1, p. 3; 3, p. 3; 4, p. 3; 5, p. 8; 6, p. 3, 7, and 8; 11, p. 6; 13, p. 7; 16, p. 6; 18, p. 6; 20, p. 2; 27, p. 3; Mar: 4, p. 6; 5, p. 6 and 8; 6,p. 3 and 11; 13, p. 8; 20, p. 4 and 6; 22, p. 6; 23, p. 6; 27, p. 6 and 7; Apr: 2, p.3; 3, p. 8; 6, p. 6; 8, p. 6; 9, p. 6; 10, p. 7; 15, p. 3; 16, p. 6; 17, p. 7; 24, p. 4; 27, p. 6; 28, p. 6; 29, p. 6; May: 1, p. 7 and 8; 3, p. 6; 8, p. 2; 15, p. 7; 22, p. 3; June: 1, p. 3; 5, p. 3; 12, p. 4; 19, p. 3; 26, p. 3; 30, p. 3; Jul: 3,p. 3; Aug: 7, p. 3; Sept: 3, p. 8; 4, p. 3; 7, p. 3; 11, p. 3; 13, p. 3; 15, p. 6;18, p. 12; 20, p. 6; 25, p. 3; Oct: 2, p. 3; 4, p. 6; 9, p. 4; 11, p. 8; 13, p. 6; 16, p. 8; 20, p. 8; 23, p. 3; 30, p. 8; Nov: 6, p. 3; 13, p. 4; 20, p. 3; 22, p. 4; 23, p. 5; 27, p. 8; 29, p. p. 3 and 6; 30, p. 6; Dec: 1, p. 6; 4, p. 3; 11, p. 7; 18, p. 7.

1911: Jan: 1, p. 3 and 4; 8, p. 3; 13, p. 6; 14, p. 6; 15, p. 3 and 6; 17, p. 3 and 6; 18, p. 3 and 6; 19, p. 6; 20, p. 3

and 6; 22, p. 3; 28, p. 8; 29, p. 3; <u>Feb</u>: 5,p. 8; 10, p. 3; 12, p. 7; 14, p. 6; 19, p. 4 and 6; 21, p. 3 and 8; 22, p. 3; 23, p. 3 and 8; 24, p. 6; 26, p. 3; <u>Mar</u>: 1, p. 3; 5, p. 3; 12, p. 3; 14, p. 8; 15, p. 6; 17, p. 6; 19, p. 4; 21, p. 3; 22, p. 3 and 6; 23, p. 6; 25, p. 6; 26, p. 4; <u>Apr</u>: 2, p. 3; 7, p. 6; 8, p. 4; 9, p. 3; 11, p. 6, 13, p. 6; 15, p. 6; 16, p. 4 and 8; 18, p. 3; 20, p. 8; 21, 6; 23, p. 3 and 4; 25, p. 6; 26, p. 6; 29, p. 3 and 6; 30, p. 3 and 8; <u>May</u>: 2, p. 6; 10, p. 6; 14, p. 8; 28, p. 3; <u>June</u>: 4, p. 3; 11, p. 3; 18, p. 3 and 6; 25, p. 8; <u>Jul</u>: 2, p. 3; <u>Sept</u>: 1, p. 3; 3, p. 3; 10, p. 3; 17, p. 4; 24, p. 4; <u>Oct</u>: 1, p. 3; 8, p. 3; 22, p. 3; 29, p. 8; <u>Nov</u>: 5, p. 8; 12, p. 3 and 6; 19, p. 4; 26, p. 8; 28, p. 8; 29, p. 3; <u>Dec</u>: 3, p. 3; 6, p. 6; 7, p. 8; 10, p. 2; 17, p. 2 and 8; 19, p. 6; 24, p. 4; 28, p. 6; 20, p. 6; 31, p. 4 and 6-7.

<u>1912</u>: <u>Jan</u>: 7, p. 3; 10, p. 6; 14, p. 8; 16, p. 6; 18, p. 6; 21, p. 3; 24, p. 8; 28, p. 3 and 6; <u>Feb</u>: 1, p. 3; 3, p. 6; 4, p. 5; 6, p. 5 and 6; 7, p. 5; 8, p. 6; 11, p.5; 18, p. 7; 25, p. 5; <u>Mar</u>: 3, p. 5; 7, p. 5; 8, p. 5; 10, p. 5; 13, p. 5; 15, p. 5; 16, p. 5; 17, p. 5 and 6; 19, p. 5; 20, p. 6; 21, p. 5; 23, p. 5; 24, p. 5; 31, p. 4; <u>May</u>: 6, p. 5; 7, p. 4; 9, p. 8; 14, p. 5; 16, p. 6; 19, p. 5; 21, p. 8; 23, p. 5; 24, p. 5 and 6; 25, p. 5 and 6; 26, p. 6; 28, p. 7; <u>May</u>: 5, p. 5; 12, p. 5; 19, p. 7; 26, p. 5; <u>June</u>: 2, p. 5; 9, p. 5; 16, p. 5; 23, p. 5; 25, p. 8; 26, p. 8; 30, p. 5; <u>Aug</u>: 30, p. 8; <u>Sept</u>: 1, p. 5; 8, p. 5; 15, p. 5 and 7; 22, p. 5; 29, p. 7; <u>Oct</u>: 6, p. 7; 13, p. 5; 20, p. 5; 27, p. 8; <u>Nov</u>: 3, p. 5; 10, p. 8; 17, p. 5; 22, p. 5; 24, p. 5; <u>Dec</u>: 1, p. 5 and 8; 7, p. 5; 15, p. 5; 19, p. 5; 20, p. 8; 22, p. 5; 24, p. 5 and 6; 29, p. 5.

<u>1913</u>: <u>Jan</u>: 12, p. 5; 19, p. 5; 26, p. 5; <u>Feb</u>: 2, p. 5; 9, p. 5; 16, p. 5; 23, p. 7; <u>Mar</u>: 2, p. 5; 9, p. 8; 16, p. 5; 23, p. 8; 30, p. 5; <u>Apr</u>: 6, p. 5; 13, p. 5; 20, p. 5; 27, p. 5; <u>May</u>: 4, p. 5; 11, p. 5; 18, p. 5; 25, p. 5; <u>June</u>: 1, p. 5; 15, p. 5; 19, p. 6; 22, p. 8; <u>Aug</u>: 14, p. 5; 21, p. 5; 27, p. 5; 28, p. 5; <u>Oct</u>: 5, p. 5; 10, p. 5; 12, p. 5; 19, p. 5; 26, p. 5; <u>Nov</u>: 2, p. 7; 9, p. 5; 16, p. 5; 23, p. 5; 30, p. 5; <u>Dec</u>: 7, p. 5; 10, p. 5; 13, p. 5; 14, p. 5 and 7; 16, p. 5; 21, p. 4; 28, p. 8.

<u>1914</u>: <u>Jan</u>: 4, p. 4; 10, p. 8; 11, p. 8; 18, p. 5; 25, p. 5; <u>Feb</u>: 1, p. 5; 7, p. 5; 8, p. 5; 15, p. 8; 22, p. 5; <u>Mar</u>: 1, p. 5; 8, p. 8; 15, p. 5; 22, p. 15; 29, p. 7; <u>Apr</u>: 5, p. 5; 11, p.

7; 12, p. 4; 19, p. 5; 26, p. 2; <u>May</u>: 3, p. 5; 9, p. 6; 10, p. 5; 17, p. 5; 24, p. 5; 30, p. 5; <u>June</u>: 7, p. 5; 14, p. 4; 18, p. 8; 20, p. 6; 21, p. 4; 25, p. 6 and 8; 28, p. 4; <u>Sept</u>: 4, p. 8; 6, p. 4; 13, p. 5; 20, p. 5; 27, p. 5; <u>Oct</u>: 11, p. 5; 18, p. 5; 25, p. 4; <u>Nov</u>: 1, p. 2; 8, p. 5; 14, p. 5; 15, p. 5; 22, p. 5; 25, p. 6; 29, p. 4; <u>Dec</u>: 5, p. 5; 6, p. 4; 11, p. 11; 13, p 5; 19, p. 7; 20, p. 15; 27, p. 7.

<u>1915</u>: <u>Jan</u>: 3, p. 11; 10, p. 12; 12, p. 6; 16, p. 5; 17, p. 5; 24, p. 15; 31, p. 4; <u>Feb</u>: 5, p. 6; 7, p. 4; 13, p. 8; 14, p. 5; 21, p. 5; 28, p. 4; <u>Mar</u>: 4, p. 6; 7, p. 4; 14, p. 11; 21, p. 5; 28, p. 12; <u>Apr</u>: 3, p. 5; 4, p. 2; 11, p. 11; 18, p. 4; 23, p. 6; <u>May</u>: 7, p. 7; 9, p. 5; 11, p. 5; 11, p. 6; 19, p. 2; 26, p. 5; <u>Sept</u>: 2, p. 7; 5, p. 4; 12, p. 12; 19, p. 4; 30, p. 8; <u>Oct</u>: 3, p. 9; 10, p. 15; 17, p. 7; 24, p. 9; <u>Nov</u>: 7, p. 4; 13, p. 5; 14, p. 9; 21, p. 9; 28, p. 12; <u>Dec</u>: 5, p. 11; 12, p. 11; 18, 5; 19, p. 14; 23, p. 7; 25, p. 2.

<u>1916</u>: <u>Jan</u>: 1, p. 2; 9, p. 11; 16, p 13; 23, p. 10; 30, p. 2; <u>Feb</u>: 6, p. 2; 12, p. 6; 13, p. 4; 20, p. 10; 27, p. 10; <u>Mar</u>: 5, p. 7; 12, p. 11; 19, p. 12; 26, p. 11; <u>Apr</u>: 2, p. 13; 9, p. 13; 16, p. 11; 23, p. 10-11; 30, p. 10; <u>May</u>: 7, p. 10; 9, p. 5; 14, p. 16; 21, p. 13; 24, p. 5; 28, p. 10; <u>June</u>: 4, p. 10; 18, p. 13; 25, p. 11; <u>Sept</u>: 19, p. 5; 24, p. 13; <u>Oct</u>: 1, p. 10; 8, p. 12; 15, p. 12; 22, p. 12; 29, p. 12; <u>Nov</u>: 5, p. 12; 12, p. 7 and 12; 19, p. 12; 26, p. 12; 29, p. 4; <u>Dec</u>:10, p. 13; 17, p. 4 and 16; 19, p. 8; 24, p. 5 and 12; 31, p. 8.

<u>1917</u>: <u>Jan</u>: 7, p. 4; 14, p. 2; 21, p. 4; 28, p. 4; <u>Feb</u>: 4, p. 5; 11, p. 4; 16, p. 5; 18, p. 2; 25, p. 5; Mar: 4, p. 5; 11, p. 5; 18, p. 5; 25, p. 6 and 12; <u>Apr</u>: 8, p. 4 and 6; 10, p. 8; 15, p. 2; 22, p. 2; 29, p. 11; <u>May</u>: 6, p. 2; 13, p. 2; 20, p. 2; 27, p. 2; <u>June</u>: 3, p. 2; 10, p. 2; 17, p. 4 and 7; <u>Dec</u>: 2, p. 2; 9, p. 12;   16, p. 12; 23, p. 4-5; 30, p. 5.

<u>1918</u>: <u>Jan</u>: 6, p. 4; 13, p. 4; 19, p. 4 and 6; 20, p. 4; 27, p. 4; <u>Feb</u>: 3, p. 4; 10, p. 4; 17, p. 4; 24, p. 4; <u>Mar</u>: 3, p. 2; 9, p. 7; 10, p. 2; 17, p. 12; 24, p. 9; 31, p. 9; <u>Apr</u>: 14, p. 2; 21, p. 4; 28, p. 2; <u>May</u>: 5, p. 2; 9, p. 6; 11, p.6; 12, p. 2; 19, p. 2; 26, p. 4; <u>June</u>: 9, p. 4; 16, p. 4; 23, p. 4; 27, p. 6; 29, p. 8; 30, p. 4.

B33   Jewel, Edward Alden: "Manchester Annual: A Rewarding Show," *New York Times* **(1 September 1935), section 9, 9:4.**

In this review of the annual Manchester (VT) art exhibition, the critic compares Ruggles's painting style to his sense of musical expression. The article includes a photo of the composer's watercolor, "Birch in Winter."

B34   Keats, Sheila: "Reference Articles on American Composers: An Index," *Juilliard Review* **I/3 (Fall 1954), 21-34.**

This article contains a two-sentence description of Charles Seeger's article on Ruggles in the *Musical Quarterly*.

B35   _____: "American Music on LP Records: An Index - Part II," *Juilliard Review* **II/2 (Spring 1955), 31-43.**

Ruggles's recorded works to that date are listed in this discography.

B36   King, A. Hyatt: "Mountains, Music, and Musicians," *Musical Quarterly* **31 (1945), 417.**

Ruggles's *Men and Mountains* is cited in a works-list of compositions with mountain themes. The work is not discussed elsewhere in the article.

[see: W4]

B37   Kirkpatrick, John: "The Evolution of Carl Ruggles (A Chronicle Largely in His Own Words)," *Perspectives in New Music,* **volume 6, number 1 (Spring-Summer 1968), 146-66.**

This is a highly informative biographical article. It summarizes Ruggles's life from letters, and as told by the composer to John Kirkpatrick. It is filled with anecdotes and also insights into Ruggles's education with descriptions of his lessons and assignments. There are also some interesting descriptions of early works which the composer destroyed or left incomplete.

[see: all works, B83]

B38   _____: Liner notes to *The Complete Music of Carl Ruggles*. CBS Masterworks Records: M2 34591, 1980.

These notes for the first recording of Ruggles's complete published works (and a few unpublished works as well) warmly present the works and anecdotally a view of the composer's life and manner. There is also information on the performances included on the recording.

[see: W1,W2/1, W2/2, W3, W4/1, W4/2, W5, W6, W7, W8, W13, W14, W15, D1]

B39   Klemm, Eberhardt: "Carl Ruggles (1876-1972[sic]) ein anderer amerikanischer Aussenseiter," *Musik und Gesellschaft* 37 (July 1987): 370-72.

Klemm concisely presents an overview of Ruggles's music, career, and life. He favorably evaluates the music suggesting that it deserved more exposure in Germany while noting some recent German performances. He describes Ruggles's atonal procedures as "a headstrong American response to Schoenbergian expressionism." The incorrect death year is printed in the article. The article is in German.

[see: W1,W2, W3, W4, W5, W6, W7, W8, W9]

B40   Kupferberg, Herbert: "Music of Our Time," *Atlantic* 217 (May 1966), 118-120.

This introduction to Ruggles and his music is written in response to the Carl Ruggles Festival at Bowdoin College and the recent release of the premiere recording of *Sun-Treader*.

[see: W6b, D8]

B41   **Mandel, Alan R. and Nancy: "Composers to Re-Emphasize: Six Americans Who Should Not Be Forgotten,"** *Clavier*, **volume 14, number 4 (1975),   17.**

This article put forward six American composers, active since 1876, whom the author hoped would be given due consideration by concert programs preparing for the United States bicentennial celebration. The composers discussed are Charles T. Griffes, Ruth Crawford Seeger, Robert Starer, Virgil Thomson, Robert Palmer, and Ruggles. The four paragraphs on Ruggles are derived from Charles Seeger and Lou Harrison. There is also an endorsement by Mandel of the *Evocations* which he recorded.

[See: W7, D 13]

B42   **Marcus, Leonard: "Ruggles All at Once,"** *HiFi/Musical America* **18 (December 1968), 20-21,   32.**

This is a detailed review of the Ruggles Festival Held in Bennington, VT on 29 September 1968. "The unique event was the result of some friends and admirers of Vermont's 'Carl' arranging, as one of them put it, 'to let him hear it all his works at least once more." The concert included a presentation of the Governor's Award for Excellence in the Arts to Ruggles by Vermont's Governor Philip Hoff. The program featured the combined efforts of four regional orchestras and a number of prominent composers and performers. The reviewer evaluates the works individually and as a body. As a whole, he states there is a sameness and mannerism in these works which bespeaks a sense of insecurity in the composer. "Despite these reservations, the festival was a memorable one. It not only evoked an historical era, it brought into perspective the musical situation today. Anybody with the slightest interest in American music will find Ruggles's music an enlightening experience."

[see: W1b, W2/2d, W3b, W4/2f, W5j, W6d, W7i, W8c, B57, B77, Pro2]

B43   *Miami Hurricane, The.* "Famous Composer of Modern Music to Conduct Winter Seminar Here," (20 January 1938), 1.

This article in the University of Miami weekly newspaper announced Ruggles's appointment by the School of Music and described the requirements for entry into this special seminar.

[see: B85]

B44   *Music and Artists*: "Obituary," volume 4, number 5 (19717-1972), 45.

It is a brief obituary statement calling Ruggles a "composer and intransigent intellectual."

B45   *Music Educator's Journal*:. "Obituary," volume 58, number 5 (January 1972) 14.

This is a brief obituary including a quote from an earlier issue that Ruggles was the "likely successor to Charles Ives as the next discovery-after-the-fact of the musical public."

B46   *Music Journal*:. "Mood," 34 (February 1976), 49.

This is a notice of the premiere of *Mood*, which was "edited by [John] Kirkpatrick from five separate sketches by Ruggles."

[See: W10a]

B47   *Musical Times*: **"Obituary," volume 112, number 1546 (December 1971), 1205.**

This is a one-paragraph obituary of the composer.

B48   *Newsweek*: **"Carl Ruggles's Season in the Sun," 67 (7 February 1966) 80-81.**

This brief essay is a commemoration of the composer's ninetieth birthday and was written to report upon the Carl Ruggles Festival sponsored by Bowdoin College. The article describes Ruggles's career and works by excerpting lines from Virgil Thomson's keynote address at the festival and intertwining them with quotes from an interview with the composer.

[see: W6b, W13a, B80]

B49   *New York Times*: **(24 September 1933), section 10, 5:3.**

An announcement of the second Yaddo Festival programs in Saratoga Springs, NY, it tells of a performance of *Angels* on strings by the Aeolian String Quartet, "assisted by Messrs. Weiser and Stern."

N. B. At the head of the page are three photographs for which Richard Donovan and Ruggles are listed as each other.

[see: W2/1d]

B50 _____: "Lange Leads Philharmonic While Toscanini Rests," (15 March 1936), section 10, 6:3.

This is an announcement of the New York Philharmonic's upcoming concert schedule which includes the first complete performance of the enlarged score of *Men and Mountains*, given in Carnegie Hall on 19 March under Hans Lange.

[see: W4/2b]

B51 _____: "Five are Elected to Arts Institute" (10 February 1954), 36:1.

Ruggles; poets Elizabeth Bishop and Robert Lowell; painter George Grosz; and architect Eero Saarinen are announced as the year's nominees to the American Institute of Arts and Letters.

[see: B52]

B52 _____: "Franklin's Ideals Seem Lost Today: R. E. Sherwood Notes Trend Toward Suspicion—Academy of Arts Makes Awards" (27 May 1954), 25:5.

Ruggles and the other 1954 American Institute of Arts and Letters inductees are listed along with new members of the Academy of Arts and Letters. It is noted that with the honor of life membership also comes an award of $1000.

[see: B51]

B53 _____: "Library Honoring Carl Ruggles, 80" (13 October 1957), 66:3.

This is an announcement of the New York Public Library's celebration of the composer's eightieth birthday to be centered around the theme of the "upcoming premiere" of *Affirmations*, a work which was commissioned by the Louisville Symphony, but never written. The exhibition included portraits of the composer, displays of articles about him, and some manuscripts.

[see: W11]

B54 _____: **"Brandeis Gives Nabokov Its Creative Arts Award" (27 May 1964), 12:7.**

Included in the article is an announcement that Ruggles received a lifetime achievement award in the arts from Brandeis University.

B55 *Notes: The Quarterly Journal of the Music Library Association*: **"Notes for Notes (Recent Acquisitions)," volume 31, number 2 (1974), 281-282.**

"The John Herrick Jackson Music Library of Yale University (Harold E. Samuel is the Music Librarian) has acquired the following: 1) The complete musical manuscripts and papers of Carl Ruggles that were in his possession at the time of his death. The materials were purchased from the Ruggles Estate. Ruggles had asked John Kirkpatrick, Curator of Yale's Ives Collection, to be his musical executor, and it is largely this connection that has led to the purchase. Kirkpatrick, during the last decade of Ruggles's life, put most of his papers in order and will continue to work on them at Yale."

[See: C1a]

B56 **Parmenter, Ross: "3 'Grand Old Men' of Music Honored"** *New York Times* **(17 October 1958), 33:1.**

This is a review of the 16 October New York Philharmonic concert featuring the works of Ruggles (*Men and Mountains*), John Becker (*Symphonia Brevis*), and Wallingford Riegger (*Music for Orchestra*) on the first half of the program, and a performance featuring Van Cliburn in Rachmaninov's *Piano Concerto No. 3* on the second. Each work was introduced and explained by the conductor, Leonard Bernstein, who also brought the composers on stage to be recognized.

[see: W4/2d, B74, B76]

B57   *Pennysaver and Press* (Bennington, VT): "A Unique and Historic Concert and Art Show to Honor Carl Ruggles," volume 11, number 21 (18 September 1968), 1-2.

The first two pages of this weekly shoppers' guide were used to advertise a concert of Ruggles's complete works under the ægis of Bennington College at the local high school.

[see: W1b, W2/2d, W3b, W4/2f, W5j, W6d, W7i, W8c, B42, B77, Pro 2]

B58   Perle, George: "Atonality and the Twelve-Note System in the United States," *Score* 27 (July 1960),   51-66.

Perle's essay is an orderly appraisal of the development of atonal practices in American music beginning with Ives and continuing through the serial procedures in use among academic composer at the time of the article's writing. Four pages are dedicated to the music of Ruggles which suggest that Ruggles's work was a continuation of Ives's experiments. Ruggles's technique is contrasted with that of Schoenberg's period of free atonality. Cowell's introduction of the terms "dissonant counterpoint," "secundal harmony," and "secundal counterpoint" are evaluated. Perle concludes that the purposeful non-systemization in the works of Ruggles negates the likelihood of a consistent method of labeling and analyzing his procedures.

[see: W2/1]

B59   Reed, Frances: "Carl Ruggles," *Vermont Life* (Fall 1951), 7-10.

A public-interest story, this article has charming and thorough descriptions of the Ruggles home and of the composer's daily work schedule. There is also an interview with Charlotte Ruggles. Reed includes descriptions of a number of works as reviewed at their premieres. She opens by describing the premiere of *Organum* as a recent event and identifies the composer as a 73 year old Vermonter. The article was actually published two years after the first performance of *Organum*. It also features some excellent photographs by John Atherton.

[see: W2, W5, W6, W8, W8a]

B60   RePass, R.: "American Composers of Today," *London Music* 8 (December 1953), 24.

Ruggles is included in this overview of contemporary American composers.

B61   *Republican-Herald, The*: Winona, MN, 1907-18.

[see: B32, Th10, C7]

Carl and Charlotte Ruggles are mentioned briefly in the following issues of this local newspaper. Most of the entries are social pages and concert announcements for the Winona Orchestra.

1907: Jan: 26, p. 3; Feb: 9, p. 5; 23, p. 3; Mar: 21, p. 8; 30, p. 5; Apr: 3, p. 6; 5, p. 6; 6, p. 5; 6, p. 9; 12, p. 5; 20, p. 6; 25, p. 6; 30, p. 6; May: 1, p. 4; 9, p. 7; 11, p. 5; 13, p. 4; 14, p. 3; 15, p. 4; 18, p. 6; 23, p. 3; 28, p. 5; 29, p. 4; 31, p. 6; June: 1, p. 3; 13, p. 8; 15, p. 3; 22, p. 3; Aug: 31, p. 4; Sept: 9, p. 6; 10, p. 4; 14, p. 3; 15, p. 8; 16, p. 3; 21, p. 8; 26, p. 6; 28, p. 10; Oct: 5, p. 7-8; 7, p. 7; 8, p. 6 and 8; 16, p. 5; 19, p. 4; 21, p. 5 and 6; 22, p. 4; 25, p. 4; 28, p. 5; 29, p. 3; 31, p. 8; Nov: 1, p. 6; 7, p.

5; 12, p. 6; 20, p. 4; 23, p. 8; 30, p. 4; <u>Dec</u>: 2, p. 4; 7, p. 6; 14, p. 4.

<u>1908</u>: <u>Jan</u>: 4, p. 4; 7, p. 6; 14, p. 8; 22, p. 5; 25, p. 3; 27, p. 3; 29, p. 8; 30, p. 5; 31, p. 3; <u>Feb</u>: 8, p. 4; 15, p. 6; 17, p. 5; 18, p. 3; 19, p. 4; 22, p. 4; 24, p. 5; <u>Mar</u>: 4, p. 4; 7, p. 5; 14, p. 3; 24, p. 5; 25, p. 5; 28, p. 4; <u>Apr</u>: 6, p. 6; 8, p. 6; 11, p. 6; 13, p. 4; 15, p. 4; 17, p 8; 20, p. 6; 22, p. 4; 24, p. 8; 27, p. 4-5; 28, p. 6 and 8; 30, p. 6-7; <u>May</u>: 2, p. 7; 23, p. 7 and 12; 26, p. 5; 29, p. 4; <u>Jul</u>: 18, p. 4; <u>Aug</u>: 19, p. 4; <u>Sept</u>: 3, p. 7; 8, p. 5; 19, p. 5-6; 26, p. 3; 30, p. 5; <u>Oct</u>: 1, p. 5; 3, p. 6 and 9; 7, p. 6; 8, p. 6 and 8; 19, p. 5; 24, p. 9; 26, p. 4; 31, p. 9; <u>Nov</u>: 7, p. 6; 9, p. 4; 10, p. 4 and 8; 14, p. 6; 23, p. 6.25, p. 6; 26, p. 6; 30, p. 6; <u>Dec</u>: 2, p. 5; 12, p. 8; 18, p. 6; 19, p. 3.

<u>1909</u>: <u>Jan</u>: 13, p. 4; 16, p. 6; 18, p. 5; 19, p. 8; 20, p. 10; 21, p. 8; 27, p.5 and 8; 29, p. 5; 30, p. 6; <u>Feb</u>: 4, p. 6; 5, p. 4; 8, p. 5; 9, p. 5; 11, p. 6; 12, p. 5; 15, p. 5; 25, p. 5; 26, p. 3; <u>Mar</u>: 3, p. 4-5; 4, p. 6; 6, p. 4; 12, p. 5; 18, p. 5; 23, p. 6; 24, p. 6; 26, p. 5; 27, p. 5; <u>Apr</u>: 10, p. 4; 21, p. 6; 24, p. 10; 29, p. 5; 30, p. 4-5; <u>May</u>: 1, p. 4; 3, p. 6; 27, p. 6; 28, p. 5; <u>June</u>: 19, p. 4; 20, p. 5; <u>Jul</u>: 10, p. 4; <u>Aug</u>: 31, p. 10; <u>Sept</u>; 18, p. 7; 23, p. 2,5, and 8; 24, p. 2; <u>Oct</u>: 2, p. 2,4, and 6; 20, p. 6; 30, p. 6; 31, p. 4; <u>Nov</u>: 3, p. 5; 17, p. 3; 20, p. 3 and 9; 27, p. 4; 29, p. 6; 30, p. 4; <u>Dec</u>: 1, p. 6; 2, p. 4-5; 3, p. 3; 13, p. 6; 18, p. 8; 24, p. 4; 27, p. 3; 31, p. 3 and 6.

<u>1910</u>: <u>Jan</u>: 3, p. 3; 8, p. 5; 16, p. 6; 18, p. 7; 19, p. 3; 25, p. 3 and 5; 29, p. 4 and 5; 31, p. 3; <u>Feb</u>: 2, p. 3 and 7; 5, p. 4; 7, p. 4 and 5; 9, p. 8; 10, p. 7; 12, p. 4; 15, p. 3; 18, p. 2 and 4; 19, p. 5; 26, p. 4; <u>Mar</u>: 2, p. 5; 5, p. 3 and 5; 12, p. 4; 17, p. 3; 19, p. 8; 23, p. 3; 24, p. 3; 26, p. 4 and 6; 28, p. 5; <u>Apr</u>: 1, p. 3; 2, p. 4; 5, p. 7; 6, p. 6 and 10; 8, p. 3 and 7; 9, p. 6 and 7; 12, p. 8; 16, p. 3, 4 and 10; 23, p. 4; 30, p. 6 and 7; <u>May</u>: 2, p. 3; 3, p. 8; 7, p. 8; 14, p. 5; 20, p. 10; 21, p. 5; 27, p. 10; 28, p. 4; 31, p. 8; <u>June</u>: 4, p. 5; 11, p. 5; 17, p. 8; 18, p. 6; 25, p. 6; 29, p. 3; 30, p. 3; <u>Jul</u>: 2, p. 4; <u>Aug</u>: 6, p. 3; <u>Sept</u>: 2, p. 6; 3, p. 6; 10, p. 6; 12, p. 3; 13, p. 3; 15, p. 3; 17, p. 7; 19, p. 10; 24, p. 2 and 5; <u>Oct</u>: 1, p. 2; 4, p. 6; 8, p. 4; 10, p. 10; 11, p. 8; 13, p. 3; 15, p. 5; 22, p. 5; 29, p. 4; <u>Nov</u>: 5, p. 4; 12, p. 5;

14, p. 4 and 7; 19, p. 5; 22, p. 8; 26, p. 5; 28, p. 3 and 6; 30, p. 3, 6 and 7; <u>Dec</u>: 1, p. 2 and 3; 19, p. 4; 20, p. 7; 23, p. 8; 24, p. 5; 27, p. 5; 31, p. 5.

<u>1911</u>: <u>Jan</u>: 7, p. 5; 9, p. 5; 10, p. 8; 12, p. 3; 14, p. 5; 16, p. 5; 17, p. 3 and 4; 18, p. 2 and 3; 19 p. 6; 20, p. 3; 21, p. 5; 27, p. 3; 28, p. 5; 30, p. 3; 31, p. 4; <u>Feb</u>: 4, p. 6; 7, p. 3; 10, p. 3; 11, p. 5; 14, p. 3; 18, p. 7; 20, p. 8; 21, p. 3 and 5; 22, p. 3 and 8; 23, p. 3; 24, p. 5; 25, p. 5; 28, p. 3; <u>Mar</u>: 4, p. 8; 11, p. 4; 13, p. 6; 16, p. 10; 18, p. 5; 20, p. 3 and 4; 21, p. 3; 22, p. 2 and 3; 23, p. 7; 25, p. 3 and 12; 30, p. 4; <u>Apr</u>: 1, p. 8; 3, p. 5; 6, p. 8; 7, p. 3; 8, p. 4; 11, p. 4; 12, p. 7; 13, p. 3; 14, p. 5; 15, p. 5; 17, p. 5 and 6; 20, p. 6 and 10; 21, p. 6; 22, p. 4 and 5; 24, p. 3, 5 and 6; 28, p. 3 and 4; 29, p. 3 and 6; <u>May</u>: 1, p. 5 and 10; 2, p. 6; 5, p. 3; 6, p. 3; 10, p. 4; 13, p. 5; 20, p. 10; 27, p. 6; <u>June</u>: 3, p. 10; 6, p. 8; 10, p. 5; 14, p. 4; 17, p. 8; 24, p. 8; 26, p. 8; <u>Jul</u>: 1, p. 6; <u>Aug</u>: 31, p. 4; <u>Sept</u>: 2, p. 6; 9, p. 8; 16, p. 6; 20, p. 10; 23, p. 2 and 6; 30, p. 2; <u>Oct</u>: 7, p. 4 and 14; 14, p. 7; 21, p. 5; 28, p. 8; <u>Nov</u>: 4, p. 7; 11, p. 6 and 7; 18, p. 8; 20, p. 7; 25, p. 5; 28, p. 2; 29, p. 10; <u>Dec</u>: 2, p. 10; 5, p. 3; 6, p. 8; 9, p. 3 and 7; 14, p. 3; 15, p. 2; 16, p. 4 and 10; 18, p. 3; 19, p. 3; 21, p. 3; 23, p. 2 and 5; 26, p. 5; 29, p. 3; 30, p. 4 and 5.

<u>1912</u>: <u>Jan</u>: 6, p. 2; 15, p. 3; 16, p. 4; 20, p. 2 and 8; 27, p. 10; 31, p. 5; <u>Feb</u>: 1, p. 3 and 4; 3, p. 6; 5, p. 3; 6, p. 3 and 8; 7, p. 3; 8, p. 8; 10, p. 10; 17, p. 5; 24, p. 8; <u>Mar</u>: 2, p. 6; 7, p. 6; 9, p. 6; 12, p. 3; 16, p. 6; 18, p. 3 and 6; 19, p. 3; 20, p. 3 and 6; 22, p. 10; 23, p. 3; 30, p. 7; <u>Apr</u>: 1, p. 10; 5, p. 10; 6, p. 6; 8, p. 7; 11, p. 3; 13, p. 3; 19, p. 3; 22, p. 3 and 10; 23, p. 3; 24, p. 3; 25, p. 3 and 7; 26, p. 5 and 12; 27, p. 10; <u>May</u>: 4, p. 5; 11, p. 6; 18, p. 4; 25, p. 5; 27, p. 5; <u>June</u>: 1, p. 5; 8, p. 5; 15, p. 5; 22, p. 12; 24, p. 3; 27, p. 3; 29,p. 10; <u>Aug</u>: 29, p. 3; 31, p. 5; <u>Sept</u>: 7, p. 6; 14, p. 5; 21, p. 10; 28, p. 10; <u>Oct</u>: 1, p. 5; 5, p. 6; 12, p. 6; 19, p. 6; 26, p. 8; <u>Nov</u>: 2, p. 8; 9, p. 3; 16, p. 5; 21, p. 10; 23, p. 6; 30, p. 6 and 10; <u>Dec</u>: 7, p. 2, 7 and 12; 14, p. 2; 18, p. 2; 19, p. 9; 20, p. 9; 21, p. 5; 23, p. 2; 24, p. 3; 28, p. 2.

<u>1913</u>: <u>Jan</u>: 4, p. 8; 18, p. 5; 22, p. 10; 25, p. 10; <u>Feb</u>: 1, p. 5; 8, p. 10; 15, p. 5; 22, p. 10; 28, p. 8; <u>Mar</u>: 1, p. 5;

7, p. 6; 8, p. 5; 15, p. 5; 21, p. 8; 22, p. 12; 24, p. 10; 29, p. 5; Apr: 5, p. 5; 12, p. 7; 17, p. 5; 19, p. 5; 21, p. 8; 26, p. 5; May: 3, p. 7; 10, p. 12; 17, p. 3; 24, p. 4; 31, p. 5; June: 14, p. 5; 19, p. 3; 21, p. 6; Aug: 16, p. 4; 23, p. 6; Sept: 13, p. 10; 20, p. 10; 27, p. 10; Oct: 4, p. 5; 11, p. 10; 13, p. 3; 18, p. 5; 25, p. 6; Nov: 1, p. 6; 7, p. 12; 8, p. 7; 15, p. 7; 22, p. 5; 29, p. 7; Dec: 6, p. 5; 10, p. 7; 12, p. 7; 13, p. 6; 15, p. 6; 20, p. 8; 26, p. 5; 27, p. 5; 31, p. 6.

1914: Jan: 3, p. 5; 9, p. 5; 10, p. 6; 17, p. 6; 24, p. 4; Feb: 6, p. 4; 7, p. 4; 14, p. 4; 21, p. 5; 28, p. 8; Mar: 7, p. 6; 14, p. 5; 21, p. 7; 28, p. 5; Apr:4, p. 7; 11, p. 5; 18, p. 5; 25, p. 5; May: 2, p. 7; 9, p. 5 and 6; 15, p. 5; 16, p. 7; 23, p. 4; 30, p. 9; June: 5, p. 7; 6, p. 3; 13, p. 5; 17, p. 5; 20, p. 5 and 8; 24, p. 6; 25, p. 9; 27, p. 8; Sept: 4, p. 3; 5, p. 5; 12, p. 5; 19, p. 5; 26, p. 5; Oct: 9, p. 7; 10, p. 5; 17, p. 6; 24, p. 5; 31, p. 5; Nov: 7, p. 5; 13, p. 7; 14, p. 5; 21, p. 5; 25, p. 7; 28, p. 5; Dec: 2, p. 6; 5, p. 5; 12, p. 5; 18, p. 6; 19, p. 5; 21, p. 9; 26, p. 6.

1915: Jan: 2, p. 8; 9, p. 7; 12, p. 10; 15, p. 7; 16, p. 5; 23, p. 5; 30, p. 5; Feb: 6, p. 5; 12, p. 7; 13, p. 5; 20, p. 6; 27, p. 5; Mar: 6, p. 5; 13, p. 5; 20, p. 5; 27, p. 5; 31, p. 12; Apr: 2, p. 9; 3, p. 5; 10, p. 8; 17, p. 5; 24, p. 5; May: 7, p. 8; 11, p. 5; 26, p. 7; June: 28, 5; Sept: 2, p. 3; 4, p. 5; 11, p. 5; 18, p. 5; Oct: 2, p. 5; 8, p. 2; 9, p. 5; 16, p. 5; 23, p. 5; Nov: 5, p. 8; 6, p. 5; 13, p. 5 and 6; 15, p. 5; 16, p. 2 and 10; 18, p. 3; 20. p. 5; 27, p. 5; Dec: 3, p. 3; 4, p. 5; 11, p. 5; 15, p. 2. 18, p. 5; 22, p. 6; 24, p. 7 and 8; 27, p. 8; 31,p. 7.

1916: Jan: 1, p. 5; 15, p. 7; 22, p. 11; 24, p. 3; 29, p. 5; Feb: 4, p. 2; 5, p. 5; 11, p. 8; 12, p. 5; 19, p. 5 and 12; 26, p. 5; Mar: 3, p. 6; 4, p. 5; 11, p. 6; 18, p. 5; 24, p. 6; 25, p. 6; 31, p. 10; Apr: 1, p. 6; 8, p. 5; 15, p. 5; 22, p. 5; 24, p. 4; 29, p. 2; May: 6, p. 5; 13, p. 5; 20, p. 2 and 5; 27, p. 2; June: 3, p. 2; 17, p. 2; 21, p. 5; 24, p. 4 and 5; Sept: 19, p. 5; 23, p. 2; 30, p. 7; Oct: 4, p. 4; 7, p. 7; 14, p. 2; 21, p. 2; 28, p. 4; Nov: 4, p. 6; 10, p. 7; 11, p. 5; 18, p. 4; 25, p. 5; Dec: 2, p. 7; 9, p. 7; 11, p. 3; 12, p. 3; 15, p. 5; 16, p. 5; 18, p. 3; 21, p. 5; 23, p. 3 and 7.

1917: Jan: 6, p. 5; 13, p. 2; 20, p. 5; 27, p. 4 and 5; Feb:
1, p. 12; 3, p. 5; 10, p. 5; 16, p. 3; 17, p. 2; 24, p. 5;
Mar: 3, p. 5; 10, p. 5; 17, p. 5; 24, p. 7; 27, p. 6; 31, p.
7; Apr: 5, p. 10; 7, p. 4; 9, p. 8; 14, p. 4; 18, p. 4; 21, p.
4; 28, p. 5; May: 5, p. 4; 12, p. 5; 19, p. 4; 26, p. 7; June:
2, p. 5; 9, p. 4; 14, p. 5; 16, p. 4 and 5; 18, p. 8; 24, p. 2;
Dec: 1, p. 8; 8, p. 4; 11, p. 8; 14, p. 7; 15, p. 8; 22, p. 3
and 4; 25, p. 8; 29, p. 4.

1918: Jan: 4, p. 4; 5, p. 2 and 7; 12, p. 4; 26, p. 7; 29, p.
4; Feb: 2, p. 7; 9, p. 9; 16, p. 9; 23, p. 7; Mar: 2, p. 10;
16, p. 6; 23, p. 8; 30, p. 9; Apr: 13, p. 2; 20, p. 2; 29, p.
4; May: 4, p. 2; 9, p. 5; 11, p. 2 and 8; 18, p. 7; 25, p. 2;
June: 8, p. 5; 15, p. 5; 22, p. 5; 24, p. 8; 27, p. 8; 29, p.
10; Jul: 1, p. 5.

**B62   Richardson, E. P.: "Three Contemporary
Americans,"** *Bulletin for the Detroit Institute of
Art* **20:3 (December 1940): 25-26.**

This article announces the acquisition of three new
American art works by the Detroit Art Institute. The
painting by Ruggles is *Leaf Series, Number One* which is
described, but not reproduced in the bulletin. The bulletin
does not mention the performance of *Evocations*, nos. 1-3
which would be given in conjunction with the initial
display of this addition to their collection of the
composer's paintings and drawings.

[See: W7b]

**B63   Rockwell, John: "Music: Carl Ruggles:
Committee for Twentieth-Century Music Gives
Retrospective at McMillin Theater"** *New York
Times* **(20 February 1976), 18:2.**

This is a review of a concert sponsored by the Committee
for Twentieth-Century Music and given at Columbia
University. According to the reviewer, the program was
intended to renew interest in Ruggles's music, but he

states that the manner of presentation and mediocre level of the performance were not ideal for achieving that task.

B64   Rosenfeld, Paul: "New American Music," *Scribner's Magazine* **89 (June 1931), 624-632.**

Rosenfeld's essay is a colorful, informed, and personally opinionated survey of the state of American concert music. He isolates seven composers as the contemporary leaders of musical development in the Americas: Villa-Lobos, Chavez, Sessions, Copland, Roy Harris, Varèse, and Ruggles. The descriptions of Ruggles's works are poetic and generally favorable: "Childlike, violent, and prophetic, Ruggles's music has a dignity of genuineness, manliness, necessity," although he also ventures to suggest that at times the music is "labored and mathematical."

[see: W2, W3, W4, W5, W14]

B65   Rosenwald, Hans: "Contemporary Music," *Music News* **43 (March 1951), 8.**

Rosenwald's column is a collection of various thoughts on contemporary music. This edition includes a brief description of Ruggles's style: "more polished than that of Ives...seems to be more dependent upon Schoenberg." He does suggest that more of Ruggles's works should be presented to the public despite their lack of accessibility.

N.B. This is incorrectly listed under Paul Rosenfeld in a number of bibliographies.

[see: W4, W5, W6]

B66   Salzman, Eric: "Carl Ruggles: A Lifetime Is Not Too Long To Search For The Sublime," *HiFi* **17 (September 1966).**

Upon its publication, this was the most thorough biographical essay on Ruggles. Salzman very successfully integrates a chronology of the principal events in Ruggles's life with numerous anecdotes, and many quotes from an interview with the composer. Ruggles's career, personality, and works are richly and affectionately described. The article features many photos and a drawing by Rockwell Kent of the composer as Captain Ahab from his celebrated edition of *Moby Dick*. Salzman presents a contemporary discography with suggestions for new releases including performers and conductors.

N.B. Charles Seeger's name is misspelled throughout.

In this author's opinion, this is the best starting point for general research on Ruggles.

[see: W1, W2/1, W2/2, W3, W4/1, W4/2, W5, W6, W6b, W7, W8, W9, W12, D4, D8, D10, D12]

B67   Sanborn, Pitts: "A Glance Toward the Left," *Modern Music*, **volume 4, number 2 (1927) 24-27.**

This short essay is a fairly witty and editorial presentation of the musical directions then being explored by Ruggles, Varèse, and Cowell. Sanborn begins by noting how only a few decades before his essay, the efforts of Debussy, Reger, and Richard Strauss were perceived as a signal of the end of western music; and that with time these composers became well-loved. From this point he introduces the three radical American composers and their music, suggesting that with time audiences might grow to appreciate their "ugly and noisy" musical undertakings.

[See: W2/1, W4/1]

B68   Schonberg, Harold   C.: "Music: Ives   and Ruggles" *New York Times* **(3 March 1961), 16:3.**

This is a review of a concert honoring Ruggles and Ives with a program of their works at the Museum of Modern

Art. Schonberg praised the level of the performances and the preparation and insight of those performing.

N.B. Lionel Nowak's name is misspelled.

[see: W2/2c, W5i, W7h]

B69   Seeger, Charles: "Carl Ruggles," *Musical Quarterly* **18:4 (1932), 578-92.**

This is the first substantial article dedicated to Ruggles and his music. As the product of one of the composer's closest friends and staunchest supporters, Seeger's writing is filled with personal quotes and anecdotes, many of which have become the bases for describing Ruggles's character and personality in successive articles by other authors. Each of the works extant at that time is thoroughly examined. These descriptions of Ruggles's compositions are generally non-technical, and given within the framework of the standard literature whence it is derived. "What a great and unwieldy corpus this American Music is—great talent, great resources, great opportunities..."

This propagandistic essay has been the touchstone of research on the composer, and because of its intimacy, deserves to remain as such.

This essay has been reprinted in *American Composers on American Music*, edited by Henry Cowell. New York: Frederick Ungar Publishing Co., 1962.

[see: W1, W2/1, W3, W4/1, W5, W6, B110]

B70   _____: "On Dissonant Counterpoint" *Modern Music* **7:4 (June-July 1930), 25-31.**

This landmark essay defines the meaning of dissonant counterpoint and explores its role in the music of the avant-garde, while creating an historical framework of similar procedures in European music of the previous few decades. Seeger notes the practice of reversing the rules of dissonance and consonance within traditional counterpoint exercises as a class-room method of atonal exploration. Ruggles is not mentioned in this article, but the term and its explanation here are cited in many future studies of his music.

[see: B168]

B71 _____: **"Charles Ives and Carl Ruggles,"** *Magazine of Art* **32 (July 1939), 396-399, 435.**

Seeger presents Ives and Ruggles as the standard bearers of "fine American art music." He suggests that they have led in the creation of a new "modern" style. An interesting feature of this essay is Seeger's thoughts on Ruggles's music as viewed from the distant future.

B72 _____: **"In memoriam: Carl Ruggles (1876-1971),"** *Perspectives in New Music,* **volume 10, number 2 (Spring-Summer 1972), 171-74.**

This brief essay contains the personal reflections of one of Ruggles's closest associates. Seeger's article is a collection of thoughts on Ruggles's personality and methodology (or lack thereof) and how it shaped his life and works. Included are some interesting comparisons with Ives.

B73 **Strongin, Theodore: "Carl Ruggles Is Central Subject of 2-day Festival at Bowdoin"** *New York Times* **(24 January 1966), 27:1.**

Strongin reviews the Bowdoin College celebration of Ruggles including a summary of the addresses, panel discussion, and a notice of the concerts.

[see: W6b, B126]

B74 **Taubman, Howard: "Music: Old and New"** *New York Times* **(18 October 1958), 17:2.**

This is a review of the 17 October New York Philharmonic matinee concert repeating the program of the previous evening which featured the works of Ruggles (*Men and Mountains*), John Becker (*Symphonia Brevis*), and Wallingford Riegger (*Music for Orchestra*) on the first half of the program, and a performance featuring Van Cliburn in Rachmaninov's *Piano Concerto No. 3* on the second. Each work was introduced and explained by the conductor, Leonard Bernstein, who also brought the composers on stage to be recognized.

[see: W4/2d, B56, B76]

B75   Tenney, James C.: "The Chronological Development of Carl Ruggles's Melodic Style," *Perspectives in New Music,* volume 16, number 2 (Fall-Winter 1977), 36-69.

While James Tenney was a student at Bennington College, he served as an assistant to Ruggles. This particular essay, however, does not reflect upon that experience, but rather is a "scientific" analysis of Ruggles's melodic writing. The compositions are grouped into six chronological periods. The works are then statistically measured for melodic intervallic frequency. Using a computer for tabulation, Tenney determines that Ruggles made a steady development in his melodic conception away from consonant and triadic intervals and toward minor seconds, major sevenths, tritones, fourths, and fifths. This information is presented in a lengthy series of graphs and reinforced with supporting statements from the composer's correspondence and writings about his works by his contemporaries, Seeger and Cowell.

[see: all works]

B76   *Time*: "Lennie's Grand Old Men," 72 (27 October 1958) 54.

This is a review of a program given by the New York Philharmonic under Leonard Bernstein of Wallingford

Riegger's *Music for Orchestra*, John Becker's *Symphonia Brevis*, and Ruggles's *Men and Mountains* with the three composers present. Of Ruggles: "Last week's audience took his sweeping, spacious *Men and Mountains* with scarcely a whimper (despite Bernstein's warning about 'crazy modern music')... [Ruggles's] life illustrates the crotchety spirit of independence that animated America's musical trail blazers."

[see: W4/2d, B56, B74]

B77   _____: "Old Salt," 92 (11 October 1968), 88-89.

This article describes the composer and his works while acknowledging the festival given in his honor in Bennington, VT. There his complete works were presented on a single program to which Ruggles could listen via a loudspeaker wired to his nursing-home room. "Composer Carl Ruggles has had a writer's block for nearly all of his 92 years... Still, what Ruggles has produced is powerful, direct, dense thoroughly American music." Included also are reminiscences from Ruggles and his acquaintances.

[see: W1b, W2/2d, W3b, W4/2f, W5j, W6d, W7i, W8c, B42, B57, B77, Pro2]

B78   _____: "Obituary," 95 (8 November 1971), 98.

"Died. Carl Ruggles. 95, pioneering American composer; of heart disease; in Bennington, VT. A salty, cracker-barrel philosopher who attributed his longevity to dirty jokes ('If it hadn't been for all those laughs, I'd have been dead years ago'). Ruggles wrote out atonal works with crayon on brown wrapping paper. Though he was a notoriously slow worker and a painstaking perfectionist—only eight pieces that require a total of 90 minutes to perform survive him—his sober tone poem *Sun-Treader* is considered a modern masterwork."

B79   *Variety*:   "Obituary," 264 (27 October 1971),
79.

This is a cursory notice on the obituary page.

B80   *Winona Daily News*: "Festival in Maine: Carl
Ruggles, One-Time Winona Conductor, Given
Tribute by Critic," (17 February 1966), 9.

The author (not indicated by name) of this article finds the
news angle to be that a former resident of Winona was
featured in a *Newsweek* article [B47]. The second half of
the newspaper article is modeled on the *Newsweek* notice.
There are some brief remembrances quoted from Winona
residents who played in the local orchestra under Ruggles.
The author also states that John Kirkpatrick (then of
Cornell University) is seeking memorabilia and programs
for the formation of a collection of the composer's papers.

[see: B48]

B81   Yates, Peter: *"Sun-Treader*, the Work of an
American Radical, in Its First American
Hearing," *HiFi* 16 (April 1966) 85-86.

This review of the first recording of *Sun-Treader* focuses
on the career and significance of the composer. The review
includes an evaluation of Robert Helps's *Symphony No. 1*
which is also on this recording which was funded by the
Naumburg Foundation. The bulk of the essay is on *Sun-
Treader* which Yates describes: "The sound does not
march forward but is continually broken, a multivocal
activity too ruggedly rhythmic to be called 'prose'—too
wide-ranging for declamation. It is a continual upheaval,
but not, as one gets into it, disordered."

[see: W6, D8]

B82   Zifrin, Marilyn J.: *"Angels* - Two Views," *The
Music Review* 29:3 (August 1968), 184-96.

This is a well-organized and systematic comparison of the various versions of *Angels* (1925, 1943, 1960). Elements of form, melody, harmony, texture, counterpoint, and pitch organization are examined in each version. Zifrin clearly demonstrates the development of Ruggles's mature compositional style through the evolution of this single work.

[see: W2/1, W2/1a, W2/2, W14, B14, B24]

B83 _____: **"Interesting Lies and Curious Truths about Carl Ruggles,"** *College Music Symposium*, **19:2 (Fall 1979), 7-18.**

In this informative essay, Marilyn Zifrin attempts to set the record straight about a number of issues in Ruggles's life. As an avid storyteller, over his long life, Ruggles was able to create a vivid picture of his experiences and family history. Ms. Zifrin suggests that some of these stories had become distorted with time. Through her contact with the composer and careful research, she has been able to clarify numerous details about the composer's family and early career.

[see: W9, B37]

B84 _____: **"Carl Ruggles: Music Critic,"** *American Music Teacher*, **32 (February-March 1983), 42-46.**

Ruggles served as music critic for *The Watertown Tribune* and *The Belmont Tribune* from 27 November 1902 to 3 November 1903. Zifrin discusses this part of the composer's life and how it served as a transition in his career. She illustrates his writing style with numerous quotes from his column.

[see: A1, A2, W23, W24]

B85 _____: "Carl Ruggles and the University of Miami" *ex tempore* 4:2 (Spring-Summer 1987), 115-135.

This article presents a detailed history of Ruggles's appointment to teach a modern music seminar and composition at the University of Miami. The essay is very well documented with quotes from many correspondences between the composer and his friends in the north, as well as a number of citations from the university newspaper, *The Miami Hurricane*.

[see: W2/2a, B43, B96]

CITATIONS IN BOOKS

B86 Anderson, Ruth E.: *Contemporary American Composers: A Biographical Dictionary*, second edition. Boston: G. K. Hall and Co., 1982; 443-444.

This reference text includes a brief biographical sketch and works-list of Ruggles. The biography states that Ruggles retired to Vermont in 1947, he actually first moved there in 1924. Anderson repeats the story of *The Sunken Bell* being withdrawn because the Metropolitan Opera wished to construct a papier-mâché bell rather than casting a special one as the composer wished.

[see: W9, B6]

B87 Apel, Paul H.: *Music of the Americas North and South*. New York: Vantage Press, 1958; 141.

This is a poorly written, disorganized book which is filled with errors. Paragraph-long biographical entries of musicians in the Americas are grouped by country, but within those groups they are in neither alphabetical, nor chronological order. To compound the difficulties created by this disarrangement, there is also no index. For Ruggles there is a very short biographical statement.

N. B. This text incorrectly states that Ruggles graduated from Harvard University. *Sun-Treader* and *Portals* are misspelled.

B88   *ASCAP Biographical Dictionary*, **fourth edition. New York: Jaques Cattell Press, 1980; 434.**

This reference work includes a brief biographical sketch of Ruggles.

B89   *ASCAP Symphonic Catalog*, **third edition. New York: R.R. Bowker Co., 1977; 399.**

This guide to commercially available orchestral music lists titles, instrumentation, timings, and publishers for each composer. No instrumentation for *Vox clamans in deserto* is given; but *Men and Angels*, and the orchestral version of *Evocations* are included.

[see: W3, W4/2, W5, W6, W14, W15]

B90   **Austin, William W.:** *Music in the Twentieth Century from Debussy through Stravinsky.* **New York: W. W. Norton, 1966; 52, 372-374, 385, 441.**

A brief biographical essay of Ruggles appears in this standard text on twentieth-century music. A works-list includes *Exaltation* and *Men and Angels*, but not *Angels*. Of Ruggles, Austin states: "The excellent musicians who know Ruggles best esteem him very highly... But the present writer can only believe that these men's judgement is warped by their sympathy for the composer's character and his ideal. To this writer, Ruggles's letters to Kirkpatrick indicate extreme vagueness of musical imagination and narrowness of interests in the world, while his music seems the inspired groping of a dilettante ex-violinist."

B91   Bauer, Marion: *Twentieth-Century Music*. New York: G. P. Putnam, 1947.

This general text includes a brief description of Ruggles and his works within a survey of American composers who did not study abroad. The composer is described as "differing completely in method and individuality... reflecting an American spirit."

B92   Bigelow, Edwin and Nancy H. Otis: *Manchester, Vermont: A Pleasant Land Among the Mountains*. Manchester, VT: The Town of Manchester, 1961.

Ruggles is among the notable residents (along with John Atherton, Dorothy Canfield Fischer, and Norman Rockwell) discussed in this book on the quaint Vermont hamlet.

B93   *Bio-Bibliographical Index of Musicians in the United States of America from Colonial Times*, second edition. Washington, DC: Music Section, Pan-American Union, 1956.

This research tool lists thirteen bibliographic sources for Ruggles from a list of approximately one hundred standard music reference books of the time.

B94   Bloom, Julius, editor: *The Year in American Music: September 1946-May 1947*; 21, 170, 217.

This text is a survey of musical activity for one concert season. For Ruggles, Bloom lists a performance of *Evocations* at the Second Yaddo Festival, and a performance of *Organum* for piano four-hands on a program of the New Music Society.

[see: W7, W8, W16a]

B95   *BMI Orchestral Program Survey, 1967-68 season.* **New York: Broadcast Music Inc., 1968.**

This survey listed all reported performances of orchestral music during that season.

B96   **Brockway, Thomas P.:** *Bennington College: In the Beginning.* **Bennington, VT: Bennington College Press, 1981; 117, 154, 155.**

In his history of the early years of Bennington College, Brockway notes a campus exhibit of 15 of Ruggles's paintings in April 1936 sponsored by the visual arts department. There is also a description of the selection of the first chair of music at the college, which Ruggles desired, and for which he was rejected.

[see: B85]

B97   **Broder, Nathan: "Carl Ruggles," in** *Musik Geschichte und Gegenwart.* **Kassel, Bärenreiter Verlag, 1963,   volume 11.**

This monumental reference includes a brief biography with a complete works-list and an evaluation of Ruggles's music, stating that: "Although Ruggles's work is small, it is held high by critics for its value." There is also a cursory bibliography. The entry is written in German.

B98   **Bull, Storm:** *Index to Biographies of Contemporary Composers*, **with supplements Metuchen, NJ: Scarecrow Press, 1964; 653.**

This lists bibliographic information of composer's biographies in general reference texts. Seven sources are listed for Ruggles.

B99   Burbank, Richard: *Twentieth-Century Music*. **New York: Facts on File Publications, 1984.**

This chronology of musical events lists the performances of six of Ruggles's works, but does not include his death. Citations are found under: 7 December 1924, 15 October 1927, 25 February 1932, 24 November 1949, 24 January 1966, and 2 February 1971.

[see: W6a, W15a]

B100   Butterworth, Neil: *A Dictionary of American Composers*. **New York: Garland Press, 1984; 397-399.**

This reference work presents a detailed biography of Ruggles with a description of the works. Butterworth concludes that the works may not be as significant as purported by Ruggles's advocates. There is an odd reference to Ruggles's introduction of a 21-note scale, which is probably meant to indicate that the composer did not treat sharp and flat enharmonic spellings of pitches as if they were identical.

[see: W1, W2/2, W3, W4/1, W4/2, W5, W6, W7, W8]

B101   *Catalogue of Published Concert Music by American Composers*, second edition, Angelo Eagon, editor. Metuchen, NJ: Scarecrow Press, 1969; 184, 224, 246, 268, 274, 292; second supplement: 118.

This reference work catalogues American compositions in print by genre. Seven works of Ruggles are listed including the orchestral version of *Evocations*.

[see: W2/2, W3, W4/2, W5, W6, W8, W15]

B102   Chase, Gilbert: *America's Music*, **second edition. New York: McGraw-Hill, 1966; 576-578.**

This general text on American music history includes a brief essay on Ruggles entitled "A Rugged Individualist." Chase provides a brief biography and description of Ruggles's works. There are well-worn quotes from Lou Harrison and Henry Cowell and a brief evaluation by Chase: "One recognizes an uncompromising integrity and a creative force that seems genuine though limited, and perhaps one deplores the lack of sensuous appeal. Yet the music stands there, as solid as Vermont granite, indifferent to our romantic inclinations, and one admires it either very much or not at all."

B103   Claghorn, Charles Eugene: *Biographical Dictionary of American Music*. **West Nyack, NY: Parker Publishing, 1973; 386.**

This reference book includes a brief biographical sketch of Ruggles.

B104   Clarke, Garry E.: *Essays on American Music*. **Westport CT: Greenwood Press, 1977.**

There is no essay on Ruggles in this collection, but there is a quote from a letter to Carl and Charlotte from John Kirkpatrick upon the death of Ives.

B105   Clough, F. F. and G. J. Cuming: *World's Encyclopedia of Recorded Music*, **third supplement. London: Sidgwick and Jackson Ltd., 1953-5.**

Columbia ML-4986 is listed in this general discography.

[see: D4]

B106   Cohn, Arthur: *Recorded Classical Music: A Critical Guide to Compositions and Performances.* New York: Schirmer Books, 1981.

The best available recordings of the repertoire, as critiqued by Cohn, are presented for each composer by work. *The Complete Works of Carl Ruggles* and Alan Mandel's recording of *Evocations* are reviewed.

[see: D1, D13]

B107   Cooper, Martin: *The Modern Age, 1890-1960.* London: Oxford University Press, 1974; 584, 596-7, 610.

In this general history text from *The New Oxford History of Music* series, Ruggles is briefly discussed as a member of the American radicals. Cooper describes him as "a minor composer of some interest... It is questionable that his tiny output of works has exerted much influence."

B108   Cope, David: *New Directions in Music*, sixth edition. Dubuque, IA: Brown and Benchmark, 1993; 78, 375, 376.

Cope lists the following of Ruggles's works as examples in the development of "soundmass" composition, and suggests recordings (as indicated): *Angels* (D2), *Lilacs* (D4), *Portals* (D4), and *Sun-Treader* (D3) . In an appendix of composer biographies, two composers, Mario Davidovsky and Elliott Carter, are compared to Ruggles, but he is not listed independently.

B109   Copland, Aaron: *The New Music, 1900-1960.* New York: W. W. Norton, 1968; 105.

In this text, Ruggles's name occurs in a list of "'older' composers who came into their own in the 1920s."

B110   Cowell, Henry, editor: *American Composers on American Music: A Symposium*. Palo Alto: Stanford University Press, 1933; 14-35.

This landmark collection of essays on American music includes Charles Seeger's essay, "Carl Ruggles."

It has been reprinted: New York: Frank Ungar Publishing Co., 1962.

[see: B69]

B111   _____: *New Musical Resources*. New York, New Music Press, 1930; second edition, 1969.

This compendium of modern compositional devices and sound sources discusses Ruggles in a section on dissonant counterpoint. In this examination, his techniques are compared with those of Schoenberg, Webern, and Hindemith.

B112   _____, and Sidney Cowell: *Charles Ives and His Music*. New York: Oxford University Press, 1955; 103, 104, 106.

In this biography of Ives, Ruggles is discussed for his involvement in Henry Cowell's (author of the book) New Music Society. The text includes a re-telling of a performance of *Men and Mountains* with which Ives's *Three Places in New England* was premiered.

[see: W4/1b]

B113   Crawford, Richard, P. Allen Lott, and Carol J. Oja: *A Celebration of American Music: Words and Music in Honor of H. Wiley Hitchcock*. Ann Arbor, MI: University of Michigan Press, 1990; 409, 419, 445, 478.

Ruggles is discussed in the following two essays in this Festschrift:

—Tick, Judith: "Dissonant Counterpoint Revisited: The First Movement of Ruth Crawford's String Quartet 1931."

Crawford's techniques of pitch organization are contrasted with those of Ruggles. Crawford's awareness of Ruggles's contrapuntal procedures is evidenced in a correspondence between her and Charles Seeger.

—Garland, Peter: "James Tenney: Some Historical Perspectives."

Ruggles's music is cited as an influence upon Tenney's early compositional style. Interestingly, the friendship between the two composers is not discussed.

B114   Daniel, Oliver: *Stokowski: A Counterpoint of View*. New York: Dodd, Mead, and Company, 1982; 524, 526, 545, 551, 553.

This large biography of Stokowski indicates a number of concerts with various orchestras upon which Stokowski programmed *Organum*, including the premiere. There is no description of the work, nor of the performances

[see: W8a]

B115   Daniels, David: *Orchestral Music: A Handbook*, second edition. Metuchen, NJ: Scarecrow Press, 1982; 250-251.

This useful reference book provides instrumentation, timings, and publishers for orchestral works listed by composer. There are subsequent cross referencing lists by duration and instrumentation making it a valuable aid to concert programming.

N.B Ruggles's death date is incorrectly listed as 1968.

[see: W2/2, W4/1, W4/2, W5, W6, W8]

B116   Demuth, Norman: *Musical Trends in the Twentieth Century.* **London: Rockcliff Publishers, 1952; 249.**

Demuth groups Ruggles with Varèse and Antheil as: "The actual twentieth-century American composers [who] have indeed been in the maelstrom of contemporary thought, but they have not actually contrived anything permanent."

[see: W2/1, W14]

B117   Deri, Otto: *Exploring Twentieth-Century Music.* **New York: Holt, Rinehart and Winston, 1968.**

In this general text, Ruggles is listed among the American experimental composers along with Ives, Varèse, and Cowell.

B118   Duke, Vernon: *Listen Here! A Critical Essay on Music Depreciation.* **New York: Ivan Obolensky, Inc., 1963.**

This collection of thoughts on the course of music in the twentieth century is particularly interesting because its author lived a dual life as a composer of serious concert music, being associated with Prokofieff, and as a writer of popular songs, encouraged by Gershwin. Duke became a friend of Ruggles during the 1920s as he associated with the New York avant-garde. Ruggles is mentioned in the context of his reflections on this period in his life.

B119   Eagon, Angelo, editor: *A Catalogue of Published Concert Music by American Composers,* **second edition. Metuchen, NJ: Scarecrow Press, 1969; 184, 224, 246, 268, 274, 292.**

See description under B101.

B120   Edmunds, John and Gordon Boelzner, editors: *Some Twentieth-Century American Composers. A Selective Bibliography*, 2 volumes. New York: The New York Public Library, 1959; volume 2, 49-50.

This collection of bibliographies of composers lists eighteen reference sources on Ruggles.

B121   Edwards, Arthur C., and W. Thomas Morrocco: *Music in the United States*. Dubuque, IA: William C. Brown, 1968.

This general text on American musical history includes a brief biographical sketch of Ruggles and a description of his works.

B122   Ewen, David: *American Composers Today: A Biographical and Critical Guide*. New York: H. W. Wilson, 1949; 28-209.

In his biographical essay on Ruggles, Ewen describes the composer's home and his daily routine. Also included is a works-list and citations of some performance.

B123   _____: *Composers Since 1900: A Biographical and Critical Guide*. New York: H. W. Wilson, 1969; 482-484.

This book possesses a concise biography of Ruggles which is well-organized and thorough including quotes from Henry Cowell and Lou Harrison.

[see: W2, W4, W5, W6, W8, W9]

B124   _____: *Music Comes to America*. New York: Thomas Y. Crowell, 1942, revised 1947; 289.

Ruggles is mentioned in a list of teaching composers (referring to his appointment at the University of Miami) in a discussion of the financial trials of solely composing concert music for a living. Ewen appears to be unaware that this appointment was merely supplemental income, and that Ruggles possessed an annuity which gave him the freedom to be just a composer, a freedom which Ewen was suggesting to be an impossibility for the composers he was describing.

B125   _____: *American Composers.* 1982; 549-552.

Within this biographical dictionary, the entry for Ruggles describes most of the published works and some of the unpublished as well. The biography is concise, but very useful with a works-list.

[see: W1, W2, W4, W5, W6, W7, W8, W13, W15, D1]

B126   _____: *The World of Twentieth-Century Music.* **Englewood Cliffs, NJ: Prentice-Hall, 1969.**

In this general reference work there is a short biography of Ruggles with a works-list and description of his compositional style including a quote from Strongin. Ewen discusses Ruggles's role in American musical history as well as his association with Ives.

[see: W1, W2/1, W14, B73]

B127   **Feder, Stuart: *Charles Ives "My Father's Song": A Psychoanalytic Biography.* New Haven, CT: Yale University Press, 1992; 320, 325, 341, 344, 346.**

This is a highly detailed research project on Ives, which brings together a vast array of source material in an attempt to psychoanalyze the composer. Much is read into why Ives did everything, but it includes a lot of useful material.

Feder presents information on Ruggles's influence on Cowell to invite Ives to submit works to *New Music Edition*. There are also accounts of social contacts between the Ives and Ruggles families.

[see: W4/1, W4/1b, W6]

B128   Garland, Peter, editor: *Soundings: Ives, Ruggles, Varèse*. Berkeley: Soundings Press, 1974.

This is an anthology of previously published essays on these three composers.

[see: B25, B26, B27]

B129   _____: *Soundings: A Lou Harrison Reader*. Berkeley: Soundings Press, 1974.

This is a collection of writings about and by Lou Harrison containing poems, doodles, music, correspondence, and essays. Harrison's essays include "Ruggles, Ives, Varèse (pp. 16-17)" and "About Carl Ruggles (pp. 39-45)."

[see: B25, B26, B27]

B130   _____: "James Tenney: Some Historical Perspectives."

See: Crawford, Lott, and Oja [113]

B131   Gleason, Harold, and Walter Becker: "Carl Ruggles," *Twentieth-Century American Composers*, Music Literature Outlines, series four (Bloomington, IN, revised February 1981), 165-169.

This is a very valuable tool for beginning research on a number of American composers. The chapter on Ruggles presents an chronological outline of his life, a works-list and analytical outline of his compositional style and procedures, and a very thorough bibliography.

[see: all works]

B132   Goss, Madeleine: *Modern   Music-Makers: Contemporary American Composers.* **New York: E. P. Dutton, 1952; 49-60.**

This is a delightful general text on twentieth-century American composers. For each composer, Goss includes a biographical essay, a photo, a quote from the composer, and a facsimile incipit of the composer's manuscript. In the Ruggles entry the works are discussed in the context of commentary quoted from contemporary concert reviews, an interview with the composer, and anecdotal exclamations from concert goers. The incipit for Ruggles is the opening of *Men and Mountains.*

There is a reprint available: Westport, CT: Greenwood Press, 1970.

[see: W1, W2/1, W2/1a, W2/2b, W3, W4/1, W4/2, W4/2a, W5, W5a, W5b, W6, W6a, W7, W8, W8a, W9, D7]

B133   Greenfield, Edward, Robert Layton, and Ivan March: *The Complete Penguin Stereo Record and Cassette Guide.* **Middlesex, England: Penguin Books, 1984; 892.**

This general record guide includes a very favorable review of the recording, *The Complete Works of Carl Ruggles.*

[see: D1]

B134   Griffiths, Paul, and Marilyn J. Zifrin: "Carl Ruggles" in *The New Grove Dictionary of Music* *and Musicians*, edited by Stanley Sadie. London: Macmillan, 1980.

When it first appeared, the biographical portion of the Ruggles entry was the most thorough to be written after the composer's death. It includes a bibliography and a clear description of the principal works and the composer's techniques.

[see: all works, B135]

B135   _____, and Marilyn J. Zifrin: "Carl Ruggles" in *The New Grove Dictionary of American Music and Musicians*, edited by H. Wiley Hitchcock. London: Macmillan, 1986.

This article is an expansion of the entry above [B134]. The most significant improvement is a substantially enlarged and updated bibliography.

[see: all works, B134]

B136   _____: *A Concise History of Avant-Garde Music from Debussy to Boulez*. New York: Oxford University Press, 1978; 34, 54, 55, 114.

In this succinct study on experimental music, Ruggles is mentioned with Ives as an American who developed atonal practices independent of the Second Viennese School. Also included are Ives's remarks at the premiere of *Men and Mountains*, and a photo of the cover for Ives's *Lincoln the Great Commoner* which was designed by Ruggles.

[see: W4/1b]

B137   Hall, Charles J.: *A Twentieth-Century Musical Chronicle: Events 1900-1988*. New York: Greenwood Press, 1989; entries: 1907f, 1917f, 1921i, 1924i, 1926i, 1932i, 1938d, 1971b.

Hall presents a chronological listing of musical events. For Ruggles, he includes the move to Winona, the composition of four works, the appointment to the University of Miami, and his death.

[see: W2/1, W4/1, W5, W6]

B138   Hipscher, Edward Ellsworth: *American Opera and Its Composers, 1871-1948*. New York: Presser, 1954; reprinted by Da Capo Press, 1978; 370-371.

This study of American opera includes a biographical sketch of Ruggles, listing *The Sunken Bell* among his works. Of Ruggles, Hipscher writes, "As a composer he is best known for his songs." This is a particularly odd comment since the two vocal compositions among Ruggles's eight principal works are the least-often performed.

[see: W9]

B139   Hitchcock, H. Wiley: *Music in the United States: A Historical Introduction*. Englewood Cliffs, NJ: Prentice-Hall, 1969; revised edition, 1974; 184.

In this basic text on American musical history, Hitchcock gives a brief description of Ruggles (whom he compares with Ives) and his music in connection with Henry Cowell's *New Music Edition*.

B140   _____, and Stanley Sadie, editors: *The New Grove Twentieth-Century American Masters: Ives, Thomson, Sessions, Cowell, Gershwin, Copland, Carter, Barber, Cage, Bernstein*. New York: W. W. Norton, 1987; 16, 18, 106.

This book is a compilation of the biographies from *The New Grove Dictionary of American Music and Musicians* (edited by H. Wiley Hitchcock. London: Macmillan, 1986) for the composers whose names are listed in the title. In the Ives biography, John Kirkpatrick discusses Ives's friendship with Ruggles. In the biography of Henry Cowell by Bruce Saylor and William Lichtenwanger, Ruggles's *Men and Mountains* is mentioned for its appearance in the first issue of *New Music*.

B141   _____, **and Vivian Perlis, editors:** *An Ives Celebration*. **Urbana, IL: University of Illinois Press, 1977; 7, 82, 207.**

This text is a collection of essays, reviews, interviews, and transcripts from panel discussions on topics centered around Ives. An early performance of *Men and Mountains* is described.

[see: W4/1b, W5]

B142   **Horn, David:** *The Literature of American Music in Books and Folk Music Collections: A Fully Annotated Bibliography*. **Metuchen, NJ: Scarecrow Press, 1977; entries: 27, 257, 277, 278, 284, 298, 331, 344, 364.**

This is an annotated bibliography which includes citations for Ruggles as noted.

[see: B143]

B143   _____, **and Richard Jackson:** *The Literature of American Music in Books and Folk Music Collections: A Fully Annotated Bibliography, First Supplement*. **Metuchen, NJ: Scarecrow Press, 1988; entries: 159, 165, 167, 169, 194.**

This is a continuation of the annotated bibliography above including citations for Ruggles as noted.

[see: B142]

B144   Howard, John Tasker: *Our American Music*, **fourth edition. New York: Thomas Y. Crowell, 1966;   398-399.**

In this general text on music in the United States, there is a brief description of his works and an excerpt from an interview on his compositional method.

B145   _____: *Our Contemporary Composers.* **New York: Thomas Y. Crowell, 1941;   241-243, 256, 326, 328.**

In this text, Ruggles is described in a section entitled "Unicorn and Lion," he being the former and Ives the latter. Howard includes quotes on the composer from Charles Seeger and Henry Cowell. Ruggles is also mentioned for his association with the Pan-American Association of Composers and the International Composers' Guild.

B146   _____, and George Kent Bellows: *A Short History of Music in America.* **New York: Thomas Y. Crowell, 1967;   265.**

This introductory book gives a brief biographical sketch of Ruggles and a description of his style, "Much of his music is austere, yet no one can doubt his honesty and integrity."

B147   Hutcheson, Ernest: *The Literature of the Piano: A Guide for Amateur and Student,* **second edition, revised. New York: Alfred A. Knopf, 1948;   363.**

This handbook on repertoire for piano by the former dean and President of Juilliard lists *Evocations* in an appendix cataloguing piano works by American composers.

[see: W7]

B148   **Kaufmann, Helen L.:** *From Jehovah to Jazz: Music in America from Psalmody to the Present Day*. **New York: Dodd, Mead, and Co., 1937; 199-200.**

This is a general overview of American music with no index. There is a short discussion of Ruggles and his music: "... a composer who, to a number of watchful contemporaries, has given evidence of an original talent sufficient to class him as a genius."

[see: W2/1, W2/1a, W4/1, W5, W6, W14]

B149   **Kennedy, Michael, editor:** *The Oxford Concise Dictionary of Music*, **third edition. New York: Oxford University Press, 1980; 550.**

The biographical entry for Ruggles in this useful reference book includes *Polyphonic Composition* among his principal works.

N. B. *Vox clamans in deserto* is listed as a choral composition. There is no chorus in this composition although this error appears in a number of sources.

[see: W12]

B150   **Kerman, Joseph:** *Contemplating Music: Challenges to Musicology*. **Cambridge, MA: Harvard University Press, 1985; 156.**

In an essay on Charles Seeger and the rise of ethnomusicology as a discipline in this collection of diverse musicological writings, Ruggles is mentioned as a friend of Seeger's from within the circle of the New York avant-garde.

B151   **Kingman, Daniel:** *American Music: A Panorama,* **second edition. New York: Schirmer Books, 1990; 455, 529-531, 537, 547.**

This is a text book which includes projects and activities for further study in the areas covered. For Ruggles, there is a short biographical sketch with a general discussion of the works. He is compared with Ives and grouped into "The American Five" with Ives, Cowell, Riegger, and Becker. This nickname occurs elsewhere; it is a response to Virgil Thomson's coining of the "American Commandos" for Copland, Harris, Schuman, Barber, and Diamond.

[see: W1, W2/1, W2/2, W3, W4/1, W4/2, W5, W6, W7, W8, W9]

B152   **Kinsella, Hazel G.:** *American Index to the Musical Quarterly.* **Washington, DC:** *Musical Quarterly,* **1958.**

This index lists articles in *Musical Quarterly* by subject. There are three which discuss Ruggles.

[see: B12, B36, B69]

B153   **Kirkpatrick, John, editor:** *Charles E. Ives, Memos.* **New York: W. W. Norton and Co., 1972; 12, 16, 21, 90, 135, 140, 141, 164, 240, 277, 280.**

As suggested by its title, this is literally a collection of memos on a wide range of topics written to or for people by Ives. These short writings address issues of daily life and of music. Included are memories of concerts and reflection upon works which he composed or had heard. It is heavily annotated and cross-referenced. Pages of memos which involve Ruggles or his works, or are written to him, are listed in the citation above.

B154   Krummel, D. W., Jean Geil, Doris J. Dyer, and Deane L. Root: *Resources of American Music History*. Urbana, IL: University of Illinois Press, 1981; entry numbers: 76, 195-A, 195-C, 227-D, 234, 239, 823, 1061-A, 1580.

This is an annotated research guide useful for many facets of American-music research. In addition to providing an annotated bibliography, there are lists of library, museum and other research sources, including descriptions of holdings, hours, and phone numbers.

[see: C1a, C1b, C2, C3, C4, C5, C6, C7, C8]

B155   Lang, Paul Henry, editor: *One Hundred Years of Music in America*. New York: G. Schirmer Books. 1961; 31.

In an essay, "The Evolution of the American Composer," by Nathan Broder, in this collection of writings on music in the United States, Ruggles is mentioned in a list of avant-garde composers.

B156   Leichtentritt, Hugo: *Music of the Western Nations*. Cambridge, MA: Harvard University Press, 1956; 287-288.

In this general history text, Ruggles and his music are described briefly: "He is a visionary, embodying the passionate Puritan energy of his ancestors and despising academic regulations and conservative traditions."

N. B. Ruggles is labeled as a "native" of Vermont. Although he resided there for nearly fifty years, he was a native of Massachusetts.

[see: W2/1, W4/2, W5]

B157   _____: *Serge Koussevitsky. The Boston Symphony Orchestra and the New American Music*.   **Cambridge, MA: Harvard University Press, 1946; 155.**

In this study of the remarkable repertoire of new music championed by Koussevitsky, Leichtentritt describes a body of music which the conductor rejected: " The extreme stubborn individualism of those strange old Yankee musicians Carl Ruggles and Charles E. Ives did not attract him."

[see: B201, B205]

B158   **Leslie, George Clarke, editor:** *The Gramophone Shop Encyclopedia of Recorded Music*. **New York: Simon and Schuster, 1942; 388.**

This general record guide includes a review of New Music Quarterly Recording 1013 featuring *Toys* and the second movement of *Men and Mountains*.

[see: D7]

B159   **Luening, Otto:** *The Odyssey of an American Composer: The Autobiography of Otto Luening*. **New York, Charles Scribner's Sons, 1980; 239, 352, 382, 451, 470.**

In these memoirs of the important composer/conductor and former head of the Bennington College music department, there are a number of personal anecdotes of Luening's contact with Ruggles. He recalls reviewing sketches of *The Sunken Bell* in anticipation of a premiere in its near future. Luening also describes Ruggles's lively and often off-color visits to Bennington College as a guest lecturer, and pleasant social exchanges between the Luenings and Ruggleses.

[see: W9]

B160   Machlis, Joseph: *Introduction to Contemporary Music*, second edition. New York: W. W. Norton, 1979; 579-581.

This text which is an overview of modern music includes a thorough, though fairly non-technical, description of Ruggles's compositional style. Machlis states: "There is a visionary quality in his music, a burning intensity. He has well been called an apostle of ecstasy."

N. B. Machlis describes *Vox clamans in deserto* as a work for solo voice, chorus, and chamber orchestra. There is no chorus in this composition although this error appears in a number of sources.

B161   Magnusson, Magnus, editor: *Cambridge Biographical Dictionary*. Cambridge, England: Cambridge University Press, 1990; 1273.

This collection of short biographies include a biographical sketch of Ruggles.

N. B. This entry includes the incorrect statement that the Winona Symphony Orchestra was founded by Ruggles in Massachusetts. It was in Minnesota.

B162   Martin, William R. and Julius Drossin: *Music of the Twentieth Century*. Englewood Cliffs, NJ: Prentice-Hall, 1980.

This is a general text on twentieth-century music which compares Ruggles to Ives and discusses the former's role in Cowell's *New Music Edition*.

B163   Mead, Rita: *Henry Cowell's New Music 1925-1936: The Society, the Music Editions, and the Recordings*. Ann Arbor, MI: University of Michigan Press, 1981.

A very thorough and well organized history of Cowell's legacy, it includes correspondence, financial records, reviews of concerts, a survey of the editions, discussions of corrections, contracts, and much behind-the-scenes information. Citations are as follows:

Ruggles: 14-15, 23, 24, 29, 35, 38, 43, 46, 49, 55, 59, 63, 139, 162, 192, 194, 213, 214, 221, 239, 355; general works: 51, 76-77, 81, 123, 137, 147, 177, 190, 206, 218, 269, 272, 282, 382, 383; Angels: 9, 41, 44, 45, 65, 71, 72, 76, 77, 81, 82, 139, 140, 256, 257, 263, 357; Evocations: 369-370, 375; Lilacs: 52, 72, 76, 77, 139-140, 263, 267-272, 357; Men and Mountains: 9, 42, 64, 69, 72, 76, 77, 89, 97, 135, 139, 194, 357; Organum: 325; Portals: 9, 43, 71, 76, 77, 139-140; Sun-Treader: 194, 205, 226, 230, 232, 234, 256, 293, 295-298, 385, 426; Toys: 71, 140, 267-272.

[see: W1, W2/1, W2/2, W3, W4/1, W4/1a, W4/2, W5, W6, W6a, W7, W8, W14, D7]

B164   Mellers, Wilfrid: *Music in a New Found Land: Themes and Developments in the History of American Music*. **New York: Alfred A. Knopf, 1965; 65-71, 74, 79, 81, 84, 93, 122, 123, 124, 127, 129, 130, 132, 135, 144, 148, 177, 178, 183, 188.**

In this standard text on American music, Ruggles is given a thorough and loving treatment. Mellers draws a number of parallels between Ruggles and Schoenberg without confusing the clear differences in their compositional processes. He compares the whys of their respective atonalities rather than the hows. There is also an interesting comparison between *Men and Mountains* and Delius's *Song of the High Hills*. Mellers discusses the stylistic similarities and constraints of all of Ruggles's principal works except *Sun-Treader*, which had yet to receive an American premiere.

[see: W2/1, W2/2, W4, W5, W7, W8, B206]

B165   **Morgan, Robert P.:** *Twentieth-Century Music: A History of Musical Style in Modern Europe and America.* **New York: W. W. Norton, 1991; 297, 314.**

In this introductory history of music in the twentieth century, Morgan includes Ruggles in two lists: one of progressive composers who did not use "exotic" musical materials; and the other, prominent members of the International Composers' Guild. Ruggles's works, however, are not discussed.

B166   **Morris, Harold:** *Contemporary American Music.* **Houston, TX: Rice Institute Pamphlets, 1934.**

This pamphlet appears in some early bibliographies of Ruggles; unfortunately, a copy could not be found for this study.

B167   **Myers, Rollo H., editor:** *Twentieth Century Music: A Symposium.* **London: Calder and Boyars, 1968;   233.**

In this collection of essays, Ruggles is mentioned in conjunction with Ives in "Music in the United States" by Robert Layton.

B168   **Nicholls, David: In** *American Experimental Music: 1890-1940.* **Cambridge: Cambridge University Press, 1990; 1-3, 97-104, 133, 135, 139.**

This is an overview of the experimental compositional techniques used by American composers during the five decade in the title. Of particular interest is the chapter "On Dissonant Counterpoint: The Development of a New Polyphony, Primarily by Charles Seeger, Carl Ruggles, and Ruth Crawford" on pages 89-133, which refers to, and expands upon Seeger's classic essay on the subject. Nicholls presents a formal analysis of *Sun-Treader* and a contrapuntal survey of all of the principal works. Ruggles's involvement in the New Music Society is also discussed in a chapter of Henry Cowell.

[see: W1, W2/1, W3, W4/1, W5, W6, W7, W8, B70]

B169   Oja, Carol J.: *American Music Recordings: A Discography of Twentieth-Century U. S. Composers*. Brooklyn, NY: Institute for Studies in American Music, 1982; 260-61.

This book lists all commercial recordings made of American compositions through 1982.

[see: D1, D2, D3, D4, D5, D7, D8, D9, D10, D11, D12, D13, D14]

B170   Pannain, Guido: *Modern Composers*, translated by Michael Bonavia. Freeport, NY: Books for Libraries Press, 1970; 247, 250-251.

This introductory text on twentieth-century music presents a very eurocentric view. Pannain clearly expresses his disdain for American composers: "They are throttled by their lack of adequate expression, like Ives, or deformed and fanatical like Varèse and Ruggles."

B171   Perlis, Vivian: *Charles Ives Remembered: An Oral History*. New Haven: Yale University Press, 1974; 21, 79, 124, 147, 151, 166, 172-176, 178, 185, 200, 201, 214.

This is a transcript of interviews about Charles Ives with sixty people who knew him. Among them is a short interview with Ruggles (pp. 172-176) made on 28 February 1969. This section includes photos of a letter from Ruggles to Ives congratulating him upon receiving the Pulitzer Prize, and Ives's written reply.

[see: C1b]

B172 Persichetti, Vincent: *Twentieth-Century Harmony*. New York: W. W. Norton, 1961; 63, 126, 222, 268.

This text is an introduction to twentieth-century harmonic procedures as categorized, defined, and surveyed by Persichetti, an eminent authority on compositional techniques. Works of Ruggles are listed as example of certain processes as follows: passages of *Men and Mountains*: chromatic melody with chromatic harmony, use of secundal harmony; passages of *Evocations*: "percussive use" of harmony; and all of *Evocations*: prominent free atonality.

[see: W4, W7]

B173 Peyser, Joan: *The New Music. The Sense Behind the Sound*. New York: Delacorte Press, 1971.

In this introduction to modern music, Peyser lists Ruggles as an associate of Henry Cowell and Edgar Varèse.

B174 Porter, Andrew: *Music of Three Seasons: 1974-77*. New York: Farrar Strauss Giroux, 1978; 11, 12, 21, 322.

In this collection of reviews from Porter's column in *The New Yorker*, a performance of *Organum* is mentioned in a commentary on a contemporary music festival at Juilliard. Ruggles name is also mentioned in conjunction with articles examining the Ives centennial festivities.

[see: W8]

B175 _____: *Music of Three More Seasons: 1977-1980*. New York: Alfred A. Knopf, Inc., 1981; 229, 560.

In this collection of reviews from Porter's column in *The New Yorker*, Ruggles's name occurs in a list of American composers represented on the 1978 season of the BBC Proms concerts [*Angels*].

[see: W2/2]

B176   _____: *Musical Events: A Chronicle, 1983-1986.* New York: Summit Books, 1989; 325.

In this collection of reviews from Porter's column in *The New Yorker*, he mentions a 1984-1985 season concert of the Cleveland Orchestra on tour at New York's Avery Fischer Hall opening with *Men and Mountains*.

[see: W4/2]

B177   Read, Gardner: *Thesaurus of Orchestral Devices*. London: Sir Isaac Pitman and Sons, 1953; 92, 94, 95, 96, 99,102, 103.

In this remarkable compilation of orchestrational practices, Ruggles's *Sun-Treader* is cited for its use of an extreme high range for horn, trumpet, and trombone; and extreme low range for tuba.

[see: W6]

B178   Reed, Robert Ray: *A Centennial Memorial Album*. Winona, MN: St. Paul's Episcopal Church, 13 May 1956.

This local history booklet briefly mentions Ruggles and his association with the Winona Symphony Orchestra.

B179   Reese, Gustave: "Carl Ruggles," in *Grove's Dictionary of Music and Musicians*, fifth edition, edited by Eric Blom. London: Macmillan, 1954; volume 7, 329.

This standard reference work contains an entry for Ruggles. It offers a biographical outline, a description of his compositional style, a works-list, and a short bibliography.

[see: W1, W2/1, W2/2, W3, W4/1, W2/2, W5, W6,W7, W8]

B180   **Reis, Claire R.: *Composers, Conductors and Critics*. New York: Oxford University Press, 1955; 5, 7.**

This is a collection of thoughts and reflections upon musical events during the first half of this century. It includes a thorough description of the first concert sponsored by the League of Composers which featured the premiere of *Angels*. Ruggles is also mentioned as a member of the International Composers' Guild.

[see: W2/1a]

B181   **_____: *American Composers: A Record of Works Written Between 1912 and 1932*, second edition. New York: International Society for Contemporary Music, 1932.**

This survey of American composers dedicates a page to Ruggles which presents a very brief biographical description, a list of all his published works to that date, and a listing of performers and locations for significant performances; however, no concert dates are provided.

[see: B182]

B182   **_____: *Composers in America: Biographical Sketches of Contemporary Composers with a Record of Their Works 1912-1937*. New York: Macmillan Co., 1938.**

In this revision of *American Composers: A Record of Works Written Between 1912 and 1932*, the biographical material has been expanded and a description of the works has been added, but significant performances are no longer listed.

N. B. The date for *Sun-Treader* is given as 1933. The previous edition listed 1932, which was the year of its premiere. The score was completed in 1931.

[see: B181]

B183   Riemann, Hugo: *Riemann Musik Lexikon.* **Mainz: B. Schott's Söhne, 1961.**

This dictionary entry includes a one-paragraph biographical sketch including a works-list and a cursory bibliography. Ruggles's stay in Winona is listed as 1912 only. The text is in German.

[see: B184]

B184   _____: *Riemann Musik Lexikon,* **expanded. Mainz: B. Schott's Söhne, 1975.**

The updated entry includes the composer's death and corrects his Winona dates. This entry contains a thorough list of compositions, including those which were incomplete. The bibliography is also enlarged, though not substantially. The text is in German.

[see: B183]

B185   Rockwell, John: *All American Music: Composition in the Late Twentieth Century.* **New York: Vintage Books, 1983; 16, 39, 44, 48, 64, 66, 69, 119.**

In this collection of essays on the directions being taken by recent and contemporary American composers, Rockwell uses Ruggles as an element of comparison: as an exemplary New England individualist in his examinations of Ernst Krenek and Elliott Carter, as a musical forbear for Philip Glass, and as a similarly intended recluse from the New York musical scene for Ralph Shapey.

B186   Rosenfeld, Paul: *An Hour with American Music.* **Philadelphia: J.B. Lippincott, 1929; 101-106.**

In this collection of short reflections on music, Rosenfeld, a former New York Herald music reviewer, presents a poetic and glowing evaluation of Ruggles's music. Portions of this essay are quoted in many successive articles on the composer.

A reprint of this text is available: Westport, CT: Hyperion Press, 1979.

[see: W2/1, W4/1, W14]

B187   _____: *Musical Impressions: Selections from Paul Rosenfeld's Criticisms,* **edited by Herbert A. Liebowitz.   New York: Hill and Wang, 1969; 137,   228,   230,   285-288.**

In this informative anthology, Ruggles is mentioned amid general thoughts on the future direction of American music. The collection ends with an essay on Ruggles which was taken from *By Way of Art* (see below).

[see: W4/1, W5, W14, B188]

B188   _____: *By Way of Art.* **New York: Coward-McCann, Inc., 1928.**

This collection of critical writings on music contains an essay "Carl Ruggles" which applauds the composer's "integrity and individuality" as expressed in his music.

[see: B187]

B189　Rossiter, Frank R.: *Charles Ives and His America*. New York: Liveright, 1975; London: Victor Gollancz Ltd., 1976; 119, 187, 213, 218, 219, 221-22, 223, 226, 228, 231, 252, 253, 258, 260-261, 262, 267, 268-270, 275, 276, 277, 308, 318, 370.

This biography of Charles Ives cites many of the composer's reminiscences of his friendship with Ruggles, including concerts, social visits, and correspondences.

[see: W2/1, W3, W4/1, W5, W6]

B190　Sablonsky, Irving L.: *American Music*. Chicago, IL: University of Chicago Press, 1969; 163.

This is a general text on the history of American music. Ruggles is mentioned in a discussion of the first edition of *New Music*.

[see: W4/2]

B191　Sadie, Stanley, editor: *The Norton/Grove Concise Encyclopedia of Music*. New York: W. W. Norton, 1988 (updated 1991); 649.

This music dictionary provides a short and accurate biographical sketch and works-list for Ruggles.

B192　Salzman, Eric: *Twentieth-Century Music: An Introduction*, second edition. Englewood Cliffs, NJ: Prentice-Hall, 1978; 132-133, 137, 163.

This general text on twentieth-century music discusses Ruggles in the context of American innovators: "His rare, dense, personal, chromatic music forms a distinct kind of American expressionism. Unlike the European expressionist, whose approach is psychological and often suggests anxiety and alienation, Ruggles was a visionary who strove for the sublime, always remembering that the path upwards is not a little rough and tortuous."

B193   Saminsky, Lazare: *Living Music of the Americas*. New York: Howell, Soskin and Crown, 1949; 104-105.

In this text, Ruggles is discussed within the framework of "American radicalism," in which he is compared with Ives. Of *Angels* and *Men and Mountains*, Saminsky writes: "[They] lamely use Schoenbergian paraphernalia;" and of *Evocations*: "All of it is of a cheerless, gray strain— stark, but how small!"

[see: W2/1, W4/1, W7]

B194   _____: *Music of Our Day: Essentials and Prophecies*. New York: Thomas Y. Crowell, 1932; 151.

This general text lists Ruggles within a description of New England composers.

This text has been reprinted: Freeport, NY: Books for Libraries Press, 1970

B195   Schickel, Richard: *The World of Carnegie Hall*. New York: Julian Messner, 1960; 363.

This history of Carnegie Hall lists "a Ruggles premiere [*Organum*]" in a description of the 1948-1949 concert season.

This text has been reprinted: Westport, CT: Greenwood Press, 1973

[see: W8a]

B196   Schwartz, Elliott and Daniel Godfrey: *Music Since 1945: Issues, Materials, and Literature.* New York: Schirmer Books, 1993; 8, 429.

This general text paraphrases Ives's often quoted exclamation at the performance of Ruggles's *Men and Mountains* with which Ives's *Three Places in New England* was premiered. Also Sándor Balassa's composition *Iris* is stylistically compared to the works of Ruggles and Sessions.

[see: W4/1b]

B197   Shirley, W. D.: "North America" in *Music in the Modern Age*, F. W. Sternfeld, editor. New York: Praeger Publishers, 1973; 373, 375, 379-380.

A general history text, it discusses the role of Ruggles's music in the experimental movement in American music.

B198   Slonimsky, Nicolas: *Music Since 1900*, fifth edition.   New York: Charles Scribner's Sons, 1994; 256, 265, 290-291, 335, 343, 395, 835, 1133.

Entries in this text include brief descriptions of premieres and significant concerts with short quotations from reviews. Of particular interest is Slonimsky's treatment of those concerts which he conducted. There is also a necrological entry.

B199   _____: *Baker's Biographical Dictionary of Musicians*, eighth edition, revised by Nicolas Slonimsky.   New York: Schirmer Books, 1992; 1560-1561.

This remarkable reference work provides an excellent concise biography of Ruggles. It includes a works-list with dates and locations of first performances, including those of revised versions. It is worth noting that Slonimsky, this dictionary's editor, conducted the premiere of *Sun-Treader* sixty years before the publication of this eighth edition. There is also a good selective bibliography. Of Ruggles's music, Slonimsky writes: "In his sources of inspiration, he reached for spiritual exaltation and mystic connotations, scaling the heights and plumbing the depths of musical expression."

B200   Smith, Cecil: *Worlds of Music*. Philadelphia: J. B. Lippincott Co., 1952; 266.

In this general survey of concert music, Smith groups Ruggles with Ives, Cowell, and Becker, whom he calls the American iconoclasts: "They wrote some of the most original pieces ever produced in this country."

B201   Smith, Moses: *Koussevitsky*. New York: Allen, Towne, and Heath, Inc., 1947; 338.

Smith discusses that the conductor's support of contemporary music was not catholic: "Koussevitsky has completely passed by what he called the extreme left-wing of American composer, such as Ruggles, Ives, Cowell, and Varèse."

[see: B157, B205]

B202   Thompson, Oscar, editor: *The International Cyclopedia of Music and Musicians*, tenth edition, edited by Bruce Bohle. New York: Dodd, Mead, 1975.

This music dictionary provides a biographical sketch for Ruggles with a list of works that includes dates and cities of first performances. There are also some quotes from the composer's contemporaries.

N. B. The instrumentations of *Men and Angels* and *Angels* are switched. Also, *Vox clamans in deserto* is listed as a choral work. There is no chorus in this composition although this error appears in a number of sources.

B203   **Thomson, Virgil:** *American Music Since 1910.* **New York: Holt, Rinehart and Winston, 1971; 6, 22, 23, 31-39, 40, 43, 49, 58, 60, 61, 63, 66, 170.**

Thomson's classic book on American composers includes a biographical sketch of Ruggles and a works-list. There is also a chapter dedicated to describing the composer and each of his works. Thomson evaluates Ruggles's place in the development of American music: "Ruggles's dilemma, of course, has been the perpetual dilemma of American composers. On one side lie genius and inspiration, on the other an almost complete lack of usable history... Ruggles faced the dilemma in still another way, which was to construct for himself a method for testing the strengths of musical materials and a system of building with them so complex, so at every point aware of tensile strengths and weaknesses, that by this seemingly neutral application of psychological and acoustic laws, works were constructed that are not only highly personal in content but that seem capable of resisting wear and time."

N. B. *Vox clamans in deserto* is listed as a set of four songs instead of three.

[see: W1, W2/1, W2/2, W3, W4/1, W4/2, W5, W6, W7, W8, W9, B206]

B204   _____: *Music Reviewed 1940-1954.* **New York: Vintage Books, 1967; 231, 272.**

This is a selection of Thomson's reviews from his tenure as music critic of *The New York Herald-Tribune*. It includes a review of a performance of *Angels* for the National Association for American Composers and Conductors in Times Hall led by Lou Harrison. Of this performance Thomson wrote: "Its plain nobility of expression and the utter perfection of its workmanship place Ruggles as one of our century's masters, perhaps the one among all from whom the young have most to learn just now."

[see: W2/2b, B205]

B205   _____: *Music Right and Left.* **New York: Henry Holt, 1951; 11, 104-105, 187, 188.**

This is another selection of Thomson's reviews from *The New York Herald-Tribune*, which also contains the essay on the *Angels* performance described immediately above. In an essay on Koussevitsky, Thomson bemoans that Ruggles has not been included on any of his Boston Symphony programs. Ruggles is also cited in an essay which attempts to identify Americanism in music.

[see: W2/2b, B204, B206]

B206   _____: *The Virgil Thomson Reader.* **New York: E. P. Dutton, 1981; 304, 305, 408-409, 452, 459, 460, 461, 468-474.**

This anthology of Thomson's writings includes the essay on Americanism in music [described in B205] in which Ruggles is cited. Ruggles is mentioned: in a review of Wilfrid Mellers's *Music in a New Found Land* [B164], in a comparison with Copland, and for his relationship with Ives. The chapter on Ruggles from *American Music Since 1910* is reprinted in full.

[see: W1, W2/1, W2/2, W3, W4/1, W4/2, W5, W6, W7, W8, W9, B203, B204]

B207   _____: *Selected Letters of Virgil Thomson,* **edited by Tim Page and Vanessa Weeks Page. New York: Summit Books, 1988; 236, 338.**

In this collection, a performance of *Portals* is mentioned in a letter from Thomson to John Cage (19 May 1949), and Ruggles's name is mentioned in a letter from Thomson to John Hohenberg, secretary of the Pulitzer Prize advisory board (2 December 1972).

[see: W5]

B208   Tick, Judith: "Dissonant Counterpoint Revisited: The First Movement of Ruth Crawford's String Quartet 1931."

See: Crawford, Lott, and Oja [B113]

B209   Watkins, Glenn: *Soundings: Music in the Twentieth Century*. New York: Schirmer Books, 1988; 442-443.

In this general music-history text, Ruggles's works are described and noted for their style and individuality. Ruggles's association with the International Composers' Guild and Varèse are also mentioned.

[see: W2/1, W4/1, W6]

B210   Weir, Albert E., editor: *The Macmillan Encyclopedia of Music and Musicians*. New York: Macmillan Company, 1938; 1596.

This reference book contains a brief biographical sketch and a works-list.

N. B. Among Ruggles's teachers is listed the name Crans, which appears in no other source in this study. It is probably meant to be Claus.

B211   Westrup, Jack and Frank Harrison: *The New College Encyclopedia of Music*, revised second edition. New York: Doubleday Press, 1979.

This music dictionary has a cursory and clumsy biographical entry for Ruggles.

N. B. The instrumentation listed for the first performance of *Angels* resembles that of the revised version, but is incorrect for either. "Marching Mountains" is listed as a principal work rather than as a movement from *Men and Mountains*. There is also a reference "though in Europe his output was smaller..." which makes no sense.

B212 **Wooldridge, David:** *From the Steeples and Mountains: A Study of Charles Ives.* **New York: Alfred A. Knopf, 1974; 208-209, 218-219, 222, 229, 241-243, 304, 317, 321.**

This biography of Ives includes correspondence between Ives and Slonimsky regarding the first performance of *Sun-Treader*. There are also details of Ives's involvement in the New Music Society concerts, including his attendance at an early performance of *Men and Mountains*.

[see: W4/1b, W6a]

B213 **Yates, Peter:** *Twentieth-Century Music.* **New York: Pantheon Books, 1967; 214, 261, 279-281, 288, 304.**

This general text on twentieth-century music includes a description of Ruggles's method and associates him with Ives. There is a brief reference to a correspondence between the author and Ruggles on his compositional philosophy. An unusual feature of this text is that it includes comments on Ruggles's unpublished *Flower Pieces* [W22] which the author calls *Flowers*.

[see: W22]

B214 **Young, Percy M.:** *A Critical Dictionary of Composers and Their Music.* **London: Dennis Dobson, 1954.**

This general text provides a short biographical essay of Ruggles with a description of his compositional style and a list of works.

B215 _____: and Paul Griffiths: "Carl Ruggles" in *The New Grove Dictionary of Music and Musicians*, edited by Stanley Sadie. London: Macmillan, 1980.

See listing under Griffiths, Paul [B134].

B216 Zifrin, Marilyn J. and Paul Griffiths: "Carl Ruggles" in *The New Grove Dictionary of American Music and Musicians*, edited by H. Wiley Hitchcock. London: Macmillan, 1986.

See listing under Griffiths, Paul [B135].

B217 Zuck, Barbara: *A History of Musical Americanism*, Studies in Musicology, number 19. Ann Arbor, MI: University of Michigan Press, 1980; 112.

There is no discussion of Ruggles as a composer, except for his involvement in composers' organizations. Zuck indicates that Ruggles's name appears in the list of editorial staff in the first issue (and only that issue) of the communist magazine *New Masses* (1926).

BOOK ON RUGGLES

B218 Zifrin, Marilyn J.: *Carl Ruggles: Composer, Painter, and Storyteller*. Urbana, IL: University of Illinois Press, 1994.

This is the first, and at present, only book devoted entirely to the study of Carl Ruggles. Its author has been at the center of scholarship on the composer for the past three decades. In addition to rigorous research and analysis,

Zifrin's biography is enriched by reminiscences of her numerous visits with Ruggles during his last years. The biography is basically chronological, tying together many sources including numerous original interviews and a good deal of previously unpublished material. There are analyses throughout which clearly show the development of works through many stages creating a remarkable image of Ruggles's painstaking process of revision. Unlike any of the shorter studies on his career, there are detailed accounts of his finances that reflect a degree of penury which was not to be expected because of his life-long annuity.

Zifrin's portrayal is very well balanced. She boldly suggests that much of the composer's innovation was based upon intuition rather than technical expertise: "All the analytical articles may be correct in explaining the music, but they do not explain Carl's own thinking about the music, or the way he himself put the sounds together. He worked in a totally intuitive way, by trial and error—trying out everything at the piano over and over again, then over again some more. He did not and could not analyze his music on a consciously intellectual level." This is a most informative and compelling biography which sheds much insight upon an extremely enigmatic composer.

[see: All Works, B134, B135]

UNPUBLISHED MATERIALS

Bunp1 *Journal of the Council of Winona City, 1906-14,* **at Winona City Hall, Winona, MN.**

This local history is housed in the Winona Historical Museum.

[see: C7]

Bunp2 Kirkpatrick, John. "The Evolution of Carl Ruggles," a manuscript.

Bunp3 _____.   **Notes from conversations with Carl Ruggles.**

Bunp4 Musical-Literary Society Secretarial and Financial Reports, at Winona Public Library, Winona, MN.

This includes minutes and business details of the Winona Orchestra when Ruggles served as conductor.

[see: C10]

Bunp5 *Carl Ruggles Papers: Yale University Music Library Archival Collection, MSS 26.* **Compiled by Adrienne Nesnow with music consultant, John Kirkpatrick: New Haven, CT, 1981.**

This is a catalogue of the Carl Ruggles Collection at Yale. An outline of its content can be found under the listing for that archive (C1a). Although it is not formally published, Yale University has made unbound copies available. A copy is also accessible through inter-library loan.

[see: Th5, C1a]

Bunp6 Scrapbooks and picture albums of Horace Seaton and other Winonans, at the Winona County Historical Society, Winona, MN.

These include programs and photographs from the years when the Ruggles lived in Winona.

[see: C7]

THESES AND DISSERTATIONS

Th1   Archabal, Nina Marchetti: *Carl Ruggles: Ultra-Modern Composer as Painter.* **University of Minnesota: Ph.D. dissertation, 1979.**

This dissertation is an interdisciplinary exploration of Ruggles's career as composer and painter. In it, the author attempts to evaluate the composer's life and work through his association with the New York ultramodern composers of the 1920s and within the perception and credo of art as expressed by the avant-garde movement led by Alfred Stieglitz. She also draws a relationship between the role of the International Composers' Guild to the circle which produced *Camera Work*. It is an excellent study of the artistic philosophies which governed the works and thoughts of Ruggles and his contemporaries, especially: Henry Cowell, Rockwell Kent, Leo Ornstein, Paul Rosenfeld, Dane Rudhyar, Charles Seeger, and Edgar Varèse. This is the most complete source of information on Ruggles's work in the visual arts.

One of the most striking features of this book is that there are 37 color plates; one of the first manuscript page of *Men and Mountains*, and the remaining are photos of Ruggles's paintings. Unfortunately, in reproduced copies, these images are unrecognizable.

The author's abstract is as follows:

"This thesis places Carl Ruggles (1876-1971) and other ultramodern composers associated with the International Composers' Guild within the context of a broad American avant-garde movement in the arts. This movement constitutes a striking parallel to the German expressionist movement, which centered around Kandinsky and the *Blaue Reiter* in Munich. The American avant-garde movement began in the visual arts during the 1910s and was guided by Alfred Stieglitz, who used his gallery 291 and magazine *Camera Work* as a forum to present and test coherent æsthetic theory. This theory, which could be applied to any of the arts, presumed that art had its source within the artist. Music as an inherently non-representational and expressive art was regarded as an inspiration for the other arts. The conception of art as expression tended to free artists from the confines of a single medium.

This thesis illustrates the vitality of the American expressionist perspective in the career of Carl Ruggles.

Ruggles's career is traced from his student days in Boston through his youthful career as a conductor and composer in Winona, Minnesota, his involvement with the ultramodern composers in the 1920s, and his later days as a painter. Although best known as a composer, Ruggles pursued painting as a consuming avocation. His work in both music and painting illustrates the way in which expressionism as an æsthetic theory freed artists to explore several media. Ruggles development as an American expressionist and his accomplishments as a composer and a painter are analyzed and documented."

[see: W1, W2/1, W2/2, W3, W4/1, W2/2, W5, W6, W7, W8, B28]

Th2   **Booth, Earl Walter:** *New England Quartet: E. A. Robinson, Robert Frost, Charles Ives, and Carl Ruggles.* **University of Utah: Ph. D. dissertation, 1974.**

This dissertation presents four New England iconoclasts(two poets and two composers), comparing their approaches to individualized expression, of re-evaluating traditional beliefs, abandoning traditional procedures, and transcendental explorations in their respective art forms. Booth suggests that the culture and climate of New England is integrally entwined with the individuality of its creative figures:

A portion of the author's abstract follows:

"Ives and Ruggles, like Robinson and Frost, were deeply rooted in the heritage of New England, particularly their updated Emersonian Transcendentalism. The eclectic nature of Ives's music, coupled with his concept of the Emersonian hero of organic growth, places him squarely in the New England tradition. Ruggles's reach for the "sublime" in music represents the Transcendental quest for the divine in every human being.
    Indeed, that each of the four iconoclasts--Edwin Arlington Robinson, Robert Frost, Charles Ives, and Carl Ruggles—has no 'school' in imitation of them indicates

that solitary independence representative of the New England world. In their departure from tradition, these four men take from the old to create the new, and indeed, represent the second New England Renaissance."

Th3   **Devore, Richard Owen:** *Stylistic Diversity within the Music of Five Avant-garde American Composers, 1929-45.* **University of Iowa: Ph.D. dissertation, 1985.**

This is study of five prominent composers in the American avant-garde movement: John Becker, Henry Cowell, Ruth Crawford, Wallingford Riegger, and Carl Ruggles. Ruggles is acknowledged for his individuality and contrapuntal style. This is a clear presentation of his, and the other four composers', interrelationships, and their collective contributions to the identity of American music.

The author's abstract is as follows:

"Several previous studies of the music written in the United States during the Great Depression and World War II have emphasized composers' concerns with making their music accessible to a wide public. This apparent turn toward conservative "Americanist" music has been characterized as a reaction against the active new music movement in the United States during the 1920s.
    Although this comparative conservativism was exhibited by such prominent American composers as Aaron Copland and Roy Harris, another important group essentially rejected or ignored the whole "Americanist" movement and continued to write music that can best be categorized as "avant-garde." This group, which was centered around Henry Cowell, also included John Becker, Ruth Crawford, Wallingford Riegger, and Carl Ruggles. All five of these composers, in addition to certain personal similarities in their careers, continued during at least part of this period to write strikingly radical music, much of which was published in Cowell's *New Music*.
    The first major section of this study surveys the historical background of the American avant-garde during the period before 1929. The second section examines

several of the various kinds of socioeconomic support available to these avant-garde composers: publications, recordings, radio broadcasts, live performances, prizes, and commissions. The third section consists of separate chapters on each of the five composers listed above, each containing analyses of three representative compositions from this time period and a biographical sketch. This section has three primary goals: to delineate some of the major factors that characterize the musical style of each composer, to demonstrate their individual and collective historical significance, and to show the wide stylistic differences within the music of these five remarkable avant-garde composers. Becker is shown to have been a pioneer in the use of soundmass techniques, Cowell in the use of ethnic musics and non-traditional instruments, Crawford and Riegger in the use of serial techniques, and Ruggles in the development of an original and highly personal contrapuntal style. The final chapter summarizes these composers' achievements and their position in American music history."

[see: W2/1, W3, W4/1, W5, W6, W7]

Th4   **Faulkner, Susan   *Carl Ruggles and His Evocations for Piano*.   American University: Master's thesis, 1973.**

This thesis presents the history of the composition of these four pieces including an appraisal of the different versions which were published. There is also a performing analysis of the works.

[see: W7]

Th5   **McMahan, Robert Young: *"The Sunken Bell" by Carl Ruggles*, 2 volumes. Peabody Institute of the Johns Hopkins University: D.M.A. dissertation, 1990.**

This is truly an exhaustive study of Ruggles's discarded opera. McMahan presents a very well-organized study of the Ruggles's compositional development during the period in which he worked on *The Sunken Bell*. McMahan also presents extensive information on the play's author, Hauptmann, and, in particular, the translator/librettist, Meltzer. There is a useful concordance of materials in the Yale Ruggles Collection, and most interestingly reconstructions of some sections of the score.

The author's abstract is as follows:

"From 1909 through 1927, Carl Ruggles labored over the composition of an opera. He progressed quite far in this endeavor, possibly finishing one version (now lost), but was never satisfied with later sketches and ultimately abandoned it. Extant among his papers, obtained by Yale University in 1973, are approximately one thousand holograph pages pertaining to this project, a setting of *The Sunken Bell* (*Die versunkene Glocke*), a play by Gerhart Robert Hauptmann, and translated into English by Charles Henry Meltzer, whom Ruggles chose to write the libretto.

The purpose of this thesis is to give a detailed history of Ruggles's years on the opera, to produce edited reconstructions of most of the better developed manuscripts from all five acts, and to examine his early compositional evolution through this music. To these ends, the main text is divided into four major segments: *Part I*. A general survey of Ruggles's acknowledged works, a look at his early career, and a history of his work on *The Sunken Bell*; *Part II*. A biographical sketch of Hauptmann, a discussion and synopsis of *Die versunkene Glocke*, and an exhaustive biography of Charles Henry Meltzer, including heretofore unpublished information about him; *Part III*. A description of the opera holographs preserved among the Ruggles Papers at Yale University; and *Part IV*. An examination of the musical content of the opera sketches.

Equally important to the text are five appendices which must be consulted during the reading of Parts IV and V [sic]. These include detailed information on the music holographs (including John Kirkpatrick's indices to the manuscripts), distribution of text lines among the manuscripts, libretto typescript, marked copy of the play owned by Ruggles (the 1899 Doubleday and McClure publication of Meltzer's English translation), and edited reconstructions of excerpts from the opera."

[see: W9, Bunp 5, C1a]

Th6   **Miller, Bruce Edward:** *Intervallic and Structural Cohesion in the "Sun-Treader" of Carl Ruggles.* **University of California, Los Angeles: Ph.D. dissertation, 1989.**

In this dissertation, the author presents a description of Ruggles as creator, and his struggle with concepts of the course of modern music. The history of the composition of *Sun-Treader* is explored and this is followed by an extensive analysis of the work. In his analysis, Miller first studies the intervallic procedures and the suggests that these foundational functions lead to the structure of the whole. The author suggest certain influences from Stravinsky's *Sacre du Printemps* and considers Ruggles's work to herald the compositional methods of the fifty years following his own works.

This is followed by an original composition, *The Phoenix Rising*, by Miller.

The author's abstract is as follows:

"Volume I takes a multi-faceted look at Carl Ruggles and his most ambitious work. The first part profiles the kind of person Ruggles was, a synopsis of his life up to the writing of *Sun-Treader*, the beginnings of *Sun-Treader*, and the nature of analysis. The second part analyzes the opening section of the work with particular regard to intervallic sets and concepts of unity. These concepts are related to the work as a whole to show how formal overall structure is achieved.

Volume II is a one-movement composition for large orchestra of approximately eighteen and one half minutes duration. The work is programmatic and is meant to depict various aspects of the Phoenix legend. The first part is concerned with the physical forming of the Phoenix and its eventual self-destruction. The second part is to portray the spiritual, yet secular, resurrection which characterizes the Phoenix legend."

[see: W6]

Th7   Orkiszewski, Paul Thomas: *An Analytical Overview of the Music of Carl Ruggles.* **Rice University: Master's thesis, 1988.**

This thesis includes a brief biography and introduction to the works. The body of this study presents the composer's music as atonal music grounded in traditional methods in the form of three analytical perspectives on Ruggles's compositional techniques: the first considers contrapuntal procedures and methods of melodic generation and mutation; the second is directed at the formal structures in the music, on the phrasal level and overall; and the third is a study of the harmonic systems developed from Ruggles's contrapuntal technique.

The author's abstract is as follows:

"During his career, Carl Ruggles was considered to be at the forefront of American contemporary music. His techniques of non-repetition of tones in melodic lines and the saturation of the vertical and horizontal domains with half-steps created a version of atonality which shares a philosophical basis with Schoenberg, but differs sharply in practice. Within a progressive vocabulary, Ruggles's music shows a foundation in tradition. He made use of traditional sixteenth-century guidelines for the construction and interconnection of individual lines, and his method of motivic development and variation are based in the music of the nineteenth century. Like Schoenberg, he applied the fundamental concepts of the past to his atonal vocabulary and musical ideal."

[see: W1, W2/1, W2/2, W3, W4/1, W2/2, W5, W6, W7, W8]

Th8   Peterson, Thomas E.: *The Music of Carl Ruggles*. University of Washington: Ph.D. dissertation, 1967.

This dissertation the first full-length study of Ruggles's life and works. The author provides a cursory biographical chapter followed by chapters dedicated to the analysis of each of the published works, except *Toys* and *Vox clamans in deserto*. Through the six chapters, each studying a different work, Peterson demonstrates the development of Ruggles's "mature style" and the genesis of his compositional technique. In a final chapter, the author attempts to connect Ruggles's works to those of his contemporaries, finding that he was the first American to adopt dissonant atonalism as a compositional method and that his artistic temperament, both visual and musical, led him to develop an organic approach to composition.

The author's abstract is as follows:

"As the first American composer to make dissonance the sole basis of his harmonic style, Carl Ruggles boldly pioneered the atonal idiom in this country in the 1920s and 1930s. Today, with increased interest in, and understanding of, atonal music, he has come to be increasingly regarded as a composer of merit and interest.

The present study seeks to fulfill the need for an extended discourse on the composer's music, providing a detailed discussion of each of his major works. Thus, the significant features of Ruggles's style are brought to the fore and described. For instance, curvilinear melodic writing, a consistently dissonant vertical element, and constantly fluctuating rhythm are particularly characteristic of his style. So, too, is his direct approach to the handling of artistic problems, such as the employment of parallel motion and note-trading to maintain dissonant level, or the use of simple three-part structure to solve a formal problem,

His self-imposed tendency to avoid repetition of a note until eight different notes have occurred in a line has caused him to be erroneously compared to Schoenberg in the past. The error of this view is apparent today since Ruggles applied his own principle in free and intuitive fashion, avoiding the use of *a priori* organizational schemes.

Although an individualist through and through, he has benefitted by the accomplishments of the past with his carefully wrought lines, skilful counterpoint, and consistency of style. Any external influences, however, are completely assimilated and transformed into music which is uniquely the composer's own.

Mercilessly self-critical, Ruggles rejects all that is weak or insincere in art, striving instead for artistic perfection and integrity of expression. Although his output is small as a result of this, it contains some of the most genuinely expressive music written in America."

[see: W2/1, W2/2, W4/1, W4/2, W5, W6, W7, W8]

Th9   Robison, Robert Tucker: *Carl Ruggles's "Sun-Treader"*. University of Illinois: DMA dissertation, 1991.

This study of *Sun-Treader* begins with a look at the composer through quotes of his contemporaries. This is followed by an overview of Ruggles's music and compositional techniques. There are many excerpts and works evaluated formally as well as for their pitch organization which is discussed using set-theory nomenclature. The second-half of the text is an in-depth analysis of *Sun-Treader*. The author attempts to draw connections between Ruggles's pitch selection and serial procedures. This analysis is orderly and clearly presented. It also presents a series of changes made to the final score compared to earlier versions and the last manuscript, all of which is insightful into the compositional process.

The author's abstract is as follows:

"This study examines the music of Carl Ruggles in an effort to reveal some of the ways that he uses melody, harmony, and rhythm in the articulation of form.

The study proceeds in two main parts. Part one considers Ruggles's work as a whole and attempts to identify the basic principles of form that underlie it.

Melody, harmony, and rhythm are first examined separately to define their individual characteristics within this music, and then the ways that they are combined in the molding of form are considered. This examination does not present a detailed analysis of each of Ruggles's major works, but, rather, draws examples from those works to illustrate his methods of articulating phrases, establishing cadences, creating drama, and maintaining unity and continuity of material.

"The second part takes the findings of part one and applies them in a detailed analysis of *Sun-Treader*.

The results of this study reveal a pervasive simultaneity of unity and conflict in Ruggles's work. Unity, here, is primarily the result of an elegant balancing of tonal and rhythmic materials. The highly chromatic tonal vocabulary from which both melody and harmony spring is complemented by a largely asymmetrical orientation of rhythm. The combination of these tonal and rhythmic materials creates an environment of almost continuous change. Arching melodic lines constructed on the principle of non-repetition of tone, undulating chromatic harmonic progressions and rhythms of continually varying density and complexity generate a musical wave motion that is central to the music's form.

Drama, or conflict, enters this unified environment through the introduction of resistance to the musical norm of change. Repetition, reiteration of tones, and regular progression in many guises energize form by impeding or focusing musical movement, thus offering the opportunity for the generation of tension and release.

This simultaneity of conflict and unity—suggesting the human struggle to transcend worldly limitations and grasp the ultimate unity of the cosmos—is offered as a possible key to understanding Ruggles's ideal expression: the expression in music is sublime."

[see: W6]

Th10   Saecker, Jan: *Carl Ruggles in Winona*. Winona State College: Master's thesis, 1967.

This is a copious study of Ruggles's years in Winona, MN. Sacker has presented a history of the composer's life in Winona which includes his marriage and his conducting career. There is a remarkably detailed bibliography of sources of information on Carl and Charlotte from local newspapers, city directories, concert programs, etc.

[see: B32, B61, C7, C10]

CONCERT PROGRAMS

Pro1   **Bowdoin Biennial Institute, 22 and 23 January 1966.**

[see: W6b]

Pro2   **Carl Ruggles Festival, Bennington, VT (29 September 1968).**

[see: W1b, W2/2d, W3b, W4/2f, W5j, W6d, W7i, W8c, B42]

Pro3   **New York Philharmonic Program Notes for 19 and 20 March 1936; 24 November 1949; 16-19 October 1958.**

[see: W4/2b, W4/2d, W8a]

MISCELLANY

M1   **Burt, Warren.** *Aardvarks: II: Mr. Natural Encounters Flakey Foont!* **Piano solo in memoriam, Carl Ruggles. Lingua Press, 1977**

This composition is dedicated to Ruggles's memory.

M2   **Hauptmann, Gerhart Robert:** *The Sunken Bell (Die versunkene Glocke),* **Charles Henry**

Meltzer, translator. New York: Doubleday and McClure, 1899.

This is the copy of the play which Ruggles possessed and used for his discarded opera of the same title.

[see: W9, Th5]

COLLECTIONS OF ARCHIVAL MATERIALS

C1a   **Yale University Music Library, New Haven, CT**

The Ruggles Collection is the primary repository for materials pertaining to the composer. This extensive collection has been catalogued in great detail by Adrienne Nesnow and John Kirkpatrick (Bunp5), of which this is a summary:

Music by Ruggles: The collection includes published scores, corrected editions and proofs, fair copies, revised versions, and sketches of all of the completed works. It also contains all known manuscripts of unpublished and incomplete works. The Nesnow/Kirkpatrick catalogue thoroughly cross references works which appear within varied sketchbooks. There are also some instrumental parts which include composer's and performers markings. John Kirkpatrick worked with Ruggles for a number of years in an attempt to organize his manuscripts. Scores which occur in Kirkpatrick's hand, or contain his annotations have been carefully indicated, as have the manusripts of others who assisted Ruggles over the years, or who served as commercial copyists. All known manuscripts which are housed elsewhere have been included in this collection in photocopy form.

Music by Others: 25 folders of works copied and or arranged by Ruggles; 6 folders of works in Ruggles's possession in either manuscript or photocopy thereof; 195

folders of other music in the composer's possession at the time of his death.

Artwork: 35 pieces by Ruggles; 51 pieces by others which were part of Ruggles's estate; 11 reproductions of works by others.

Correspondence and Writings: 182 folders of general correspondence to and from Ruggles; 16 folders of papers and correspondence relating to honors and awards; 3 folders of notes for lectures; 5 folders of jottings and addresses; 5 folders of financial records; 2 folders of legal papers, mostly regarding royalties and musical contracts; 21 letters of introduction and autobiographical sketches; 2 biographical sketches of others (Ives and Varèse).

Programs: 185 concert programs; 9 exhibit catalogues of art shows in which Ruggles's paintings were shown.

Newspapers and Periodicals: 208 newspaper clippings regarding works or performances by Ruggles; 168 newspaper clippings regarding works of other composers, which were saved by Ruggles; 54 newspaper clippings regarding art works of others, which were saved by Ruggles; 78 newspaper clippings regarding Ruggles's life or awards he was given; 4 newspaper clippings regarding Ruggles's son Micah; 63 newspaper clippings regarding others; 27 periodicals containing articles relevant to the composer.

Photographs: 29 of Ruggles alone; 44 of Ruggles with others; 17 family photographs; 22 of other people.

Recordings: The collection includes three recordings of Ruggles's music which were in his possession: 1 copy of the 1934 New Music Quarterly Recording (D7), and 2 copies of the Carnegie Hall in-house recording of Organum (D6).

Miscellany: books, bulletins, brochures, scrapbooks, etc.

[see: W1, W2/1, W2/2, W3, W4, W5, W6, W7, W8, W9, Q10, W11, W12, W13, W14, W15, W16, W17,

W18, W19, W20, W21, W22, W23, W24, W25, B154, Bunp5, Th5, D6, D7]

C1b   Yale University Library, New Haven, CT

The Oral History of American Music housed in Stoechel Hall includes the "Ives Project" which is comprised of sixty recorded interviews regarding Charles Ives, one of which is by Ruggles.

[see: B154, B171]

C2   Library of Congress, Washington, DC

The collection contains copies of Ruggles's principal manuscripts and some original manuscripts which include unpublished works.

[see: B154]

C3   University of Miami Music Library, Miami, FL

This collection contains a photocopy of the manuscript of *Evocations No. 4* with marginalia and corrections written in by the composer.

[see: W7, B154]

C4   Moldenhauer Archives, Spokane, WA

This collection includes a number of manuscript letters.

[see: B154]

C5   New York Public Library, New York, NY

This collection includes a number of holograph scores.

[see: B154]

C6   Smithsonian Institute, Washington, DC

This collection contains seven letters between Ruggles and Rockwell Kent regarding music notation.

The Archives of American Art "Photographs of Artists" collection includes photographs of Ruggles taken by John Atherton which are catalogued under Atherton's name on mircofilm reel 440, frames 766-771.

[see: B154]

C7   Winona County Historical Society, Winona, MN

This collection contains one manuscript page from *Men and Mountains* and assorted correspondence from 1907 to 1917. There are also photographs and programs from the Winona Symphony and a number of scrapbooks and photo albums from the years when the Carl and Charlotte Ruggles lived in Winona. They also have archival access to the local newspapers *The Independent* and the *Republican-Herald*.

[see: W4/1, B32, B61, B154, Bunp1, Bunp6, Th10]

C8   Herman Laninger, 1349 North Highland Street, Los Angeles, CA 90028

Laninger was the principal engraver for the *New Music Editions*. This collection includes paperwork and correspondence between Ruggles and that publication.

[see: B154]

C9   Bennington College Music Library, Bennington, VT

The collection in the music building, Jennings Hall, includes a copy of the in-house recording of *Organum* made at Carnegie Hall under Stokowski. The disc's container bears Ruggles's signature and a hand-written incipit of the opening theme.

[see: D6]

C10   Winona Public Library, Winona, MN

The library's archival collection includes the financial record, business meeting minutes, and selected correspondence of the Winona Symphony during Ruggles's leadership.

[see: Bunp 4, Th10]

C11   Bennington Historical Museum, Bennington, VT

The museum has the manuscript of the title page of *Portals*.

[see: W5]

INDEX

This index includes subjects, performers, composers, organizations, authors, journals, books, and articles. These are identified with the appropriate mnemonic (W, D, A, B, Th, Pro, M, C) and their respective catalogue numbers. Those references which occur in the "Biography" are indicated by page number. Subjects and performers are distinguished with bold type.

About the Author

JONATHAN D. GREEN is Director of Choirs at Elon College. An active composer, he has received commissions throughout the United States, Great Britain, and Australia. His *Conductor's Guide to Choral-Orchestral Works* was published in 1994.

Recent Titles in
Bio-Bibliographies in Music

Elinor Remick Warren: A Bio-Bibliography
Virginia Bortin

Howard Hanson: A Bio-Bibliography
James E. Perone

Peter Sculthorpe: A Bio-Bibliography
Deborah Hayes

Germaine Tailleferre: A Bio-Bibliography
Robert Shapiro

Charles Wuorinen: A Bio-Bibliography
Richard D. Burbank

Elliott Carter: A Bio-Bibliography
William T. Doering

Leslie Bassett: A Bio-Bibliography
Ellen S. Johnson

Ulysses Kay: A Bio-Bibliography
Constance Tibbs Hobson and Deborra A. Richardson, compilers

John Alden Carpenter: A Bio-Bibliography
Joan O'Connor, compiler

Paul Creston: A Bio-Bibliography
Monica J. Slomski, compiler

William Thomas McKinley: A Bio-Bibliography
Jeffrey S. Sposato

William Mathias: A Bio-Bibliography
Stewart R. Craggs